X

arthur ashe

OF
TENNIS
& THE
HUMAN SPIRIT

———— ❧ ————

MARVIN MARTIN

An Impact Biography

Franklin Watts
A Division of Grolier Publishing
New York / London / Hong Kong / Sydney
Danbury, Connecticut

This book is dedicated to
Jenna Caroline Burch and Chandler Cale Burch,
world-class grandchildren.

Frontispiece: Arthur Ashe at Wimbledon in 1969

Photographs ©: AP/Wide World Photos: 144 (Malcolm Clarke), 155 (Steve Helber), 137 (Robyn Wishna), 15, 75, 88, 103, 113; Archive Photos: 105 (Don Hogan Charles/ New York Times), 79 (Edward Hausner/ New York Times), 96 (Mark Lien/New York Times), 1, 71; ASUCLA Photography: 23, 55, 59 (Elaine Adams); Gamma-Liaison: cover (Claudio Edinger), 7 (Art Seitz), 9 (Tim Wright); Reuters/Corbis-Bettmann: 152 (Bruce Young); Robert Coscarelli: 176; Sygma: 128 (Steve Burns), 134 (Charles Steiner); UPI/Corbis-Bettmann: 27, 34, 44, 53, 63, 107, 109, 115, 121, 122, 126.n

Visit Franklin Watts on the Internet at
http://publishing.grolier.com

Library of Congress Cataloging-in-Publication Data

Martin, Marvin
Arthur Ashe : of tennis and the human spirit / by Marvin
Martin.
p. cm. — (An Impact Biography)
Includes bibliographical references and index.
Summary: Discusses the personal life and sports career of the African-American tennis champion, Arthur Ashe, as well as his struggles with racism and AIDS.
ISBN 0-531-11432-5 (lib. bdg.)   ISBN 0-531-15959-0 (pbk.)
1. Ashe, Arthur—Juvenile literature. 2. Tennis players—United States—Biography—Juvenile literature. [1. Ashe, Arthur. 2. Tennis players. 3. Afro-Americans—Biography.] I. Title.
GV994.A7M37 1999
796.342'092—dc21
[B]   98-8535
                                                    CIP
                                                    AC

© 1999 by Marvin Martin
GROLIER
PUBLISHING
All rights reserved. Printed in the United States of America
1 2 3 4 5 6 7 8 9 10 R 08 07 06 05 04 03 02 01 00 99

Contents

————— ∿ —————

Preface:
Tribute to a
Champion

——————— ✺ ———————

The moment had come, the long-awaited moment when the brand-new, shining 23,000-seat monument to the glory of tennis would be officially dedicated. It was the evening of August 25, 1997, the opening night of the U.S Open Championships, and virtually every seat was taken in this crown-jewel stadium of the United States Tennis Association (USTA) National Tennis Center in Flushing Meadows, New York. The debate over naming the new state-of-the-art facility had ended months before. It could have been named for a corporate sponsor, as so many stadiums are today, or after the USTA or one of its founders. But the USTA, which raised all the funds for construction costs privately, decided against those options.

Instead they named the stadium for the one player who best represented the highest standards of a tennis champion on and off the court. The plaque that was unveiled during the dedication ceremony that night and would permanently adorn the stadium was inscribed:

Arthur Ashe Stadium
Dedicated August 25, 1997
USTA National Tennis Center

One of the hands lifting the veil belonged to Jeanne Moutoussamy-Ashe, the widow of the tennis champion, who had addressed the crowd a few moments earlier. "Among all the things that Arthur taught us," she said, "is

5

that inclusion is what each of us seeks and deserves." She told of her husband's stand against bigotry and his intolerance of anything less than equal opportunity for all. In conclusion, she told the audience that he "saw you all as valued brothers and sisters in the family of man and included *you* in his prayers for a better world."

Earlier, USTA president Harry A. Marmion spoke of Ashe's work with the USTA, especially his role in founding the National Junior Tennis League (NJTL), a public recreational program. "This and his countless humanitarian efforts," Marmion continued, "helped define a truly extraordinary man, and in many ways set a standard against which other athletes will be judged for decades to come." When the dedication was first announced in July 1997, Marmion had called Ashe "the greatest ambassador our sport has known."

Adding to the remarks that night was one of Ashe's teammates on the Davis Cup team and one of the world's great players, John McEnroe. "Although Arthur may not be standing here among us, we take satisfaction that at this stadium, on this occasion, time was taken to honor a man who embodied the best that tennis and sports in general can provide."

A few days earlier, the new stadium had held its first scheduled event, Arthur Ashe Kids' Day. This full-day tennis festival is held annually to honor the memory of Arthur Ashe and his commitment to children. Ashe had dedicated much of his life to children's causes. In addition to NJTL, he was instrumental in the founding of several other organizations benefiting children, including the Ashe-Bollettieri Cities Program and the Safe Passage Foundation. Both organizations have a similar purpose and used a similar strategy. They use tennis to attract kids, especially inner-city kids, but teach them the things they need to know to live fruitful, productive lives. As Ashe said in his book *Days of Grace,* "Trying to be the next Michael Jordan is fine, I tell them, but why not also aim for the goal of owning the team that employs the next Michael Jordan."[1]

Jeanne Moutoussamy-Ashe and daughter, Camera, taking part in
Arthur Ashe Kids' Day in August 1997

The legacy of Arthur Ashe has been interpreted in
many ways. But his gift of inspiration and hope for the
young may certainly be among the most cherished of his
bequests. Virginia Glass, a family friend and former
American Tennis Association (ATA) president, said, "His
legacy is primarily to the youth of America, not (just)
African-Americans; he established the National Junior
Tennis League . . . primarily for underprivileged children,
whatever their race, and it is still going strong."[2]

This book tells the story of this remarkable tennis
champion and humanitarian "who loved all kids, and will
be loved always."[3]

Introduction

———— ❧ ————

Arthur Ashe, Jr., was a role model for the world. It would be a relatively simple task to merely tell about his life on the court, for it was playing championship tennis that brought him worldwide recognition. He was the first African-American male to reach that level, which had been reserved almost exclusively for whites. That is a fascinating story in itself, but it would not come close to portraying fully the person of Arthur Ashe. His influence and impact on the world went well beyond the court, reaching into areas of human society that even he may have never dreamed he would enter.

True, without tennis Arthur Ashe may not have achieved off the court as he did—his fame gave him the leverage to accomplish what he put his mind to. But what distinguishes him from other great tennis players—some more accomplished than himself—is the degree to which he used his fame for his own personal growth and for the betterment of the world around him.

Even without tennis, Arthur Ashe would have made his mark on the world, although he may not have achieved the recognition that he did as a celebrity tennis star. That he was highly intelligent, disciplined, and motivated has been well established. It was these factors, along with pure athletic ability and skill, that brought him crashing through a rigid tennis racial barrier and into the forefront of that sport.

The same characteristics that helped Arthur Ashe succeed on the court also made him an outstanding student, always placing at or near the top of his class through elementary school, high school, and college. And he never stopped being a student, carrying books and tapes with him wherever he traveled all his life. Strongly patriotic, he served as a lieutenant in the U.S. Army after college and proudly represented the United States in the Davis Cup.

Arthur Ashe would have been well remembered if his accomplishments had been confined to tennis. But he cared deeply about other aspects of life. His numerous writings, including several autobiographical books, reflect an almost insatiable need for self-expression along with a constant concern for improving the human condition. And he displayed, as well, the determination to take his concerns into action. He strove to improve opportunities for minorities, whether in the United States or abroad.

He particularly cared about children and their education. Arthur Ashe set up and sponsored tennis camps for young people but always stressed that education came first. His statue in Richmond, Virginia, shows him holding a tennis racket and books, the books higher than the racket. He also worked at improving health conditions, establishing organizations such as the Arthur Ashe Institute for Urban

The statue of Arthur Ashe that graces Richmond's
Monument Avenue

Health. The last years of his life, when he knew there was little time left, were spent in a campaign to promote greater understanding of AIDS and to martial resources for its defeat.

However, what Arthur Ashe may be best remembered for—outside of tennis—is his battle against apartheid, the institution of racial segregation in South Africa that kept millions of non-white Africans living under conditions of degradation and poverty. He was a leader in a crusade against the South African system, which included boycotts against that country's participation in international sporting events. The pressure he and others brought to bear on South Africa eventually caused apartheid to crumble, making possible a new government of full representation for the non-white majority. Fortunately, Arthur Ashe lived to see these accomplishments at the brink of realization.

When Nelson Mandela, the leader of the African National Congress, was released from a South African prison after twenty-seven years, he said that Arthur Ashe was the person he would most like to meet[1]—not only because of Ashe's anti-apartheid activities but also because Mandela was a tennis devotee. "Ashe and Mandela, who became friends, will be linked forever by their dignified responses to prejudice," said the *Chicago Tribune* in a 1997 article.[2]

Arthur Ashe wanted all the races of the world to live together in peace and harmony. He loved traveling and, through tennis, visited countries in every continent. He enjoyed learning and partaking of other cultures. His favorite T-shirt carried the inscription, "I Am a Citizen of the World." So dear was this idea to Ashe that Home Box Office channel (HBO) called their hour-long memorial of him *Arthur Ashe: Citizen of the World.*

In a memorial statement about the tennis champion, President Bill Clinton said, "Arthur Ashe never rested with fame. He used the strength of his voice and the power of his example to open the doors of opportunity for other African-Americans, fighting discrimination in America and around the world. . . . He was a true American hero and a great example to us all."[3]

1

Coming of Age in Segregated Richmond

The municipal tennis tournament at Byrd Park was coming up, and the aspiring eight-year-old tennis player and his older cousin went there to register. Young Arthur Ashe, Jr., was getting very good at this game, and he was being encouraged to move up in competition. When the boys asked to sign up, however, they were refused. Byrd Park, it seems, was for whites only, and Arthur was a black child. The year was 1951 and the place was Richmond, Virginia.[1]

Arthur's Hometown

The picturesque, historic city of Richmond, capital of Virginia, lies on the James River in the eastern part of the state. Although only about 100 miles (161 kilometers) south of Washington, D.C., it nevertheless became the capital of the Confederacy during the Civil War, and the area is steeped in the heritage of that conflict. It was besieged near the beginning of the war, but did not fall until April 1865, near the war's end, when Union forces led by General Ulysses S. Grant crushed its weakened defenses.

Richmond recovered quickly from the war's devastation and was soon rebuilt, prospering from a flourishing tobacco industry that remains a staple to this day. Despite its rather northerly location and the outcome of the war, the city remained a shining example of Southern customs and charm. Many travelers are attracted by its Southern hospitality, and it takes pride today in being a popular convention center. Visitors delight in its old Southern architecture, tree-lined streets and floral displays, fine restaurants, and historic sites. And there is modern Richmond, as well, with high-rises and shopping centers, a well-defined art community, and its own Internet site complementing the historic culture. Indeed, the city calls itself a "perfect blending of the past with the present."[2]

Richmond takes pride in its traditions, as well it should. However, one of those traditions, which remained deeply rooted until past the mid-twentieth century, was the practice of segregation. It was a social system entrenched throughout the South until the civil rights legislation of 1964 and 1968 began its dissolution. Segregation was designed to keep the races apart, particularly to separate the white race from the black race.

The signs of segregation have all but disappeared today, but as recently as the 1960s, visitors were sometimes stunned to see symbols of racism overtly displayed. Public places, such as rest rooms and drinking fountains were prominently labeled "colored" or "white." Blacks were relegated to the rear of public buses and were usually restricted to the balconies of movie theaters, although they paid the same admission price as whites. Only certain jobs were available to them, mostly menial and poorly paid.

They were forbidden to eat in the same restaurants as whites, shop in the same stores, go to the same schools, or play in the same parks. And they were not allowed to use the same athletic facilities, including tennis courts. Those facilities set aside for "blacks only" were always inferior to those for whites. This was the law of the land in the South, and those who did not abide by it could be, and often were, harshly punished. A black man could be killed for showing attention to a white woman—not legally, of course, but through the actions of private citizens or organizations such as the Ku Klux Klan, which took the law into its own murderous hands.

Into this climate of racial oppression Arthur Ashe, Jr., was born. In his lifetime, he experienced the pain of racism but lived to see the legal dismantling of segregation. However, despite the advances made against racism in succeeding years, Arthur Ashe, even while dealing with a life-threatening disease, said that being a black man in the United States was the most difficult struggle he faced day in and day out throughout his lifetime.[3]

On July 10, 1943, Arthur entered the world at St. Phillip's Hospital, Richmond's designated black medical facility.[4] So birth was Arthur's first segregated experience. And in 1943, the whole world was in turmoil. World War II raged in Europe and the Pacific, with U.S. troops once again fighting to help preserve democracy and bring freedom to the oppressed nations of the world. Arthur was a little more than two years old when the war ended in 1945.

A Colonial Ancestry

Unlike many Americans, Arthur Ashe could trace his ancestry back to colonial times—to the year 1735 when a slave ship unloaded its cargo at Portsmouth, Virginia. Among those slaves was a West African woman who was sent to a plantation where she and a male slave began the line that eventually branched into the Ashe family. Those two slaves were identified only by numbers but undoubtedly, as was the custom, took the last name of the plantation owner, Robert Blackwell. From these roots grew a family tree that was traced to the present day by Arthur Ashe's cousin Thelma.

In 1839, Jinney, a great-great-grandchild of that first couple, married a Sauk Indian called Mike. They produced a son named Hammett who married a woman named Julia Tucker from another plantation. Hammett and Julia were among the first generation of their family to experience freedom.

Hammett and Julia had twenty-three children. Their large family inspired Ashe to comment that "Freedom must have inspired Hammett and Julia Blackwell to follow the prophet's order to 'go forth and multiply.' " One of their children, Sadie, married a man named Willie Johnson, and their daughter Amelia married Everett "Pink" Ashe, whose ancestors were once owned by Governor Samuel Ashe of Virginia. In 1920, Amelia and Pink had a son, and they named him Arthur. Pink, whose name may have been derived from "Pinkham" or possibly from his skin color, left the family when Arthur was about twelve years old.

Arthur grew up around South Hill, Virginia, where his parents had settled, but shortly after Pink Ashe left he went to Richmond, where there were more work opportunities. There he became skilled in many trades, including carpentry and auto mechanics. In Richmond, Arthur met the fetching Mattie Cordell Cunningham, and the two were married in 1938. Arthur Robert Ashe, Jr., was born five years later, and his brother, Johnnie, about five years after that.[5]

Life in the Ashe Family

From the beginning, Arthur had two strong role models in his parents. They believed in fair play and discipline, characteristics that Arthur displayed throughout his life. Arthur's father, in particular, lived by certain rules. They governed his life, and he drilled them into his sons.

For a while Arthur Sr. worked part-time for several wealthy Richmond families—sometimes as chauffeur or butler, sometimes as a handyman. Arthur Jr. said later that his father was considered to have a "good job" for a black man in Richmond in those days.[6] Arthur Sr. was still just a teenager when he got a job with the city of Richmond.

A major turning point in the lives of both Arthurs came in 1947. When young Arthur was only four years old, Arthur Sr. went to work for the city of Richmond as a special policeman and was put in charge of Brook Field, a park and playground set aside for black people.

The job required the Ashe family to move from a relative's home on Brook Road to a small frame house on the grounds of Brook Field. Right outside the door of Arthur

No matter what his age, Arthur Jr. always had great respect for his dad, Arthur Sr. Here the two of them enjoy the moment after Arthur Jr.'s victory at the 1968 U.S. Open Championships.

Jr.'s new home were all the athletic facilities of the park. They included baseball fields, a swimming pool, and, most significantly, four tennis courts. "Where would I be today if there hadn't been any tennis courts near me?" Ashe later asked in his book *Advantage Ashe*.[7]

It was in the doorway of that house that Arthur Jr. remembered seeing his mother for the last time. She stood there in her blue bathrobe as young Arthur ate breakfast. "Baby," as people called his mother, went into the hospital for surgery that day and never came back. Early on a Saturday morning in March 1950, Arthur Sr. told his children that their mother had died. Arthur Jr. was only six years old. He never forgot how his father, a stern, strong man, wept that morning. According to Arthur Sr., a jaybird in a tree near the house stopped singing on that day and was never heard again.[8]

Arthur remembered very little about his mother, but he did recall that she taught him to read when he was four years old and that she taught him manners and told him a lot about angels. After his wife's death, Arthur Sr. became a single parent. He had pledged to his wife that he would raise the children himself. Having to work everyday, he hired an older woman, Mrs. Otis Berry, to take care of the children, cook, and do household chores.

Although Mrs. Berry provided some "mothering," Arthur Jr.'s father became the single greatest influence in his life. He was very strict with Arthur, but fair, and throughout his life Arthur Jr. respected no one more than his father. "The values that my father instilled in me will never go away," he wrote in his published diary, *Portrait in Motion*. "And I recognize that the possession of them made it possible for me to succeed."[9]

Arthur Sr.'s rules sometimes seemed extreme. When young Arthur started elementary school, for instance, the father walked his son to school on the first day of classes. They walked at the boy's pace, and Mr. Ashe timed the walk. Then he told Arthur he must be home every day after school in the exact number of minutes that first walk took. And not one minute later.

Mr. Ashe kept a close and watchful eye on his sons. They were kept close to home, and if they strayed or misbehaved, punishment was swift. There was no back talk. They were not allowed to take outside jobs, not even delivering newspapers, and only rarely could they participate in after-school activities. But they had chores to do at home—and no excuses if they weren't done.

"I had to keep my room at home clean. I did washing and ironing and I went to the Presbyterian Church every Sunday," Arthur would say in *Advantage Ashe*. "I said 'Yes ma'am' and 'No ma'am' to Mrs. Berry. . . ."

A Good Student

And there was no fooling around at school either. Arthur was expected to bring A's home on his report cards; B's were not acceptable. Fortunately, this was not a huge problem because Arthur was very bright, and he loved school. He did not get a B until the sixth grade, and he remembered being terrified to go home that day.[10]

Recalling those days, Ashe said, "I really was unusual. I mean from the first, I adored school. Loved it." His brother, Johnnie, was very different in temperament. He was not a good student, and he was more mischievous. This worried their father, who could not figure out why Johnnie wasn't a "good boy" like Arthur. Finally, he realized that it was Arthur who was unusual, not Johnnie. But the discipline at home also served Johnnie well; he ended up as an officer in the U.S. Marine Corps. Johnnie was also a better all-around athlete than Arthur, even by Arthur's own admission.[11]

In the Family

Johnnie and Arthur were about five years apart so there was not much sibling rivalry, and though they had quite different personalities, they got along well. As adults, they even became business partners for a while. Arthur also came to love his many aunts, uncles, and cousins, and he especially doted on his grandmother—his mother's mother—who was called "Big Mama." Big Mama had had ten children, and Amelia (Grandmother Taylor), his father's mother, had seven. At one count Amelia had more than one hundred grandchildren. So there was no lack of kin in the Ashe-Cunningham family; Arthur loved to attend their big family reunions throughout his life.

Arthur Sr. took his children everywhere with him—hunting, fishing, and even on his playground rounds (eventually he was in charge of all of Richmond's black playgrounds). He taught them all his skills too—how to use tools and work with their hands—because he thought they would need these assets to survive in a white-dominated world.

Another dimension was added to young Arthur's family life when his father quite suddenly remarried. Mr. Ashe and Lorene Kimbrough were wed in March 1955, when

Arthur was eleven. Arthur found his stepmother to be witty and charming and enjoyed being with her. He developed a close friendship with her that continued throughout his life.[12]

Not only did young Arthur have a new mother figure, but he acquired a younger stepbrother, Robert, and a stepsister, Loretta, as well. This was all a little strange at first, but as time passed, they bonded into a loving family.

The death of his mother when he was only six no doubt had a lasting impact on Arthur's life. Something else happened to Arthur at about the same time that would change forever the direction of his life. He began to take an interest in the activity at the tennis courts across the street. He decided to borrow a tennis racket and began scrambling about the courts playing with anyone he could find. He was just a small spindly kid, smacking a tennis ball with a racket almost as big as he was, but it was the beginning of a personal evolution that would change the history of tennis.

2

Entering the World of Black Tennis

The lure of the tennis courts right outside his house was hard for Arthur to resist. If he couldn't find someone to play with, he pounded the ball off a backboard. Although slight of build, he was well coordinated and quick even then. He tried to learn the fine points of the game by watching others. Sometimes he went over to restricted Byrd Park and, from a distance, watched the white kids play.

Closer to home, Arthur could observe tennis team members from nearby Virginia Union University, a black college, who played regularly on the Brook Field courts. One of those players who seemed more advanced than the others particularly caught his eye. The day they met was a fateful encounter in the life of Arthur Ashe.

Meeting Ronald Charity

Eventually, the college tennis player became curious about the kid whose eyes were glued on him. Probably young Arthur already knew that the player he was watching was Ronald Charity, arguably the best black tennis player in the city. When he heard the kid's name, Charity, who was also an instructor at the playground, knew immediately that he was the son of the playground's caretaker. Seeing Arthur's interest in tennis, Charity asked the young boy if he wanted to learn the game, and Arthur eagerly said yes. Charity soon recognized Arthur had exceptional talent and resolved to develop it.

"If the court near my house in Brook Field was the coincidence that brought me into tennis when I was very young, the divine intervention was that a young black player named Ronald Charity . . . recognized my potential. . . ." Ashe later wrote.[1]

There were few good black tennis players in Richmond in those days. The facilities for blacks were poor, and there was a lack of quality instruction and competition. It was and always had been a white person's sport, and, at its higher levels, it was largely a sport that belonged to wealthy white people. Tennis is an expensive sport. The best players had to have access to the top tennis clubs, equipment, and training, and these advantages were not then available to African-Americans in the United States. They were barred from the best clubs and from competing against the best players. Those conditions have changed, but the top rung of players are still mostly white.

Ron Charity was one of the few people at that time who wanted to promote black tennis. Arthur's enthusiasm for the game and his dedication and discipline at such an early age impressed the young instructor. Charity himself was entirely self-taught. He learned to play tennis mostly from instructional books and through sheer determination and practice.

Charity taught Arthur the proper grip and all the various strokes: forehand, backhand, volley, and serve. "We practiced crosscourt forehands, forehands down the line, crosscourt backhands," Charity said. "We played every summer evening."[2] Arthur determined to improve. When Ron Charity wasn't available, he played with other boys or hit balls against the backboard for hours. He found tennis to be something he could do on his own, like reading, which was a favorite pastime. He became so involved in workouts that he hardly thought about having friends.[3]

For his ninth birthday, Arthur asked for a new tennis racket to replace the dilapidated one he had been using. An aunt and uncle, at some personal sacrifice, got him the new racket. He had been doing well enough with the old one, however. So well that, almost from the beginning, Ron Charity wanted to enter Arthur in tournaments. The first tournament may have taken place when he was eight years old at Brook Field. Arthur played a good game but was finally beaten by an eleven-year-old. The ice was broken, however, and now he had a the taste for competition. Under Charity's guidance and training, Arthur began entering other tournaments in Richmond's blacks-only parks. And he began winning, even against older players.

Arthur was improving so fast, in fact, that he was running out of competition among the boys in the area. To raise Arthur's level of competition, Charity requested that he be allowed to join the Richmond Racquet Club. This was an all-adult, black tennis club to which Charity belonged. Against the tougher competition of grown-ups, Arthur sharpened his skills.

When Arthur was ten years old, Charity wanted to help widen his world. So young Arthur was enrolled in the junior development program of the American Tennis Association (ATA). He was entered in nearby ATA tournaments in Roanoke, Hampton, and Norfolk, picking up valuable tournament experience in his own age group.

The Tennis Color Barrier

The ATA was the black counterpart of what was then the white-dominated U.S. Lawn Tennis Association (USLTA, now USTA). ATA, founded in 1916, claims to be the oldest African-American sports organization in the United States. "The only show in town was the ATA," recalled Bob Davis, a former ATA champion who played in those junior tournaments with Arthur in the early 1950s.[5]

The color barrier in tennis had just barely been breached at that time. In 1948, Oscar Johnson became the first African-American to enter and win a USLTA-sanctioned tournament, but Althea Gibson, in 1950, was the first African-American allowed to enter the National Championships conducted by the USLTA. For most blacks at that time, however, USLTA tournament competition was closed, especially in the South.[6]

Moving Ahead

Arthur was obviously an exceptional talent in tennis, and in 1953 when Arthur was ten, Ron Charity realized he had taken the boy as far as he could. He knew that Arthur had championship potential, but he needed to move to another training level to reach that potential—especially if he were ever to compete with the well-coached and well-trained white players.

Charity was familiar with all the tennis-training opportunities available in the area, and one stood out. That was the one he wanted for Arthur. Having discussed the possibility with Arthur's father, he put in a call to Robert Walter Johnson, M.D., of Lynchburg, Virginia. Charity knew Dr. Johnson through ATA tennis, in which Dr. Johnson was prominent. Charity had even trained at times on the court built on the Johnson grounds in Lynchburg. With Arthur Sr.'s permission, Charity arranged for young Arthur to meet Dr. Johnson.

Arthur was surprised when Ron Charity told him he was going to meet a doctor. He remembers thinking, "The man was a doctor. But I wasn't sick, and the doctor wasn't planning to give me a physical. He wanted to see me play tennis."[7] It was very curious.

When Dr. Johnson first saw Arthur he was dismayed at his size. He was so skinny the doctor wondered if he could even hold a racket. Watching Arthur play, he was still not convinced of his potential, but he agreed to take on the boy. That meant two weeks at Dr. Johnson's home in Lynchburg with five or six other young African-American tennis players.

Arthur's father had always kept him close to home, but he loved Arthur and wanted what was best for him. He recognized that this was a rare opportunity for his son, and he trusted the men who were guiding him, knowing they were of the highest character. He also knew that Dr.

At first, Dr. Johnson thought Arthur was too skinny to be a great tennis player, but his build never hindered his talent.

Johnson ran a highly disciplined, no-nonsense kind of camp, a lot like Arthur's home environment. So it was with little reluctance that his father agreed to let Arthur go to Dr. Johnson's camp.

It was the summer of 1953, and Arthur Ashe's life was about to take a new direction.

3

Arthur's Incredible Expanding World

From the time he was ten until he finished high school, Arthur spent part of almost every summer training at Dr. Johnson's home in Lynchburg. During the rest of the year, he lived the life of a normal schoolboy, except that his father restricted his after-school activities, even into high school. And of course as long as the weather would permit, he could practice tennis right outside his door.

A Disciplined Upbringing

Arthur's life was very regulated. His father saw to that. "There's [to be] no hanging around," was one of his commandments. "If you don't have to be somewhere, you should be home. . . ."[1] "My children never roamed the streets. A regular schedule was very important." He laid out the rules like they were immutable laws of the universe that could not be disputed. "I don't believe in arguing and fussing. I can't stand it; never could," he stated.[2]

Growing up, Arthur's main activities included school, household chores, sometimes helping his father, and tennis practice. He participated in other sports too. Baseball fields and a swimming pool were close by. He liked football, but his father forbade him to play the sport because of his slight build. His brother Johnnie was good at tennis, winning some tournaments in ATA when he got older, but football may have been his best sport. Johnnie won high school letters in football, baseball, track, basketball, and tennis, making All-State in football and tennis. Later, while in the Marines, he made the All-Service football team and was offered a football scholarship at Duke University.[3]

Arthur loved to go to school, but chores were not his favorite thing. When he was older, Arthur's father periodically put his two sons to work on a house he was building in Gum Springs, a suburb of Richmond. Arthur looked back proudly on his father's ability to build his own house, constructed almost entirely with surplus scrap materials. But Arthur was never happy about being dragged off to do manual labor. Protesting his father's orders, however, was out of the question.[4]

Instead, Arthur would have preferred to read. Throughout his life, despite his tight schedules, Arthur always found time to read. Even between matches at a tournament, Arthur could often be found nearby reading a book. Later in life when he was a touring tennis professional, books and other reading material made up the main bulk of his luggage.

While growing up and into adulthood, Arthur read anything he could lay his hands on: books, newspapers, magazines, everything. He even loved reading the encyclopedia his father bought for him while he was in grade school. And he became particularly fond of *National Geographic* magazine after he rescued a huge collection of old issues from the garbage. Later he became a life member of the National Geographic Society. Chances are Arthur's love of reading stemmed from his mother reading to him and teaching him to read before he started school.[5]

Staying on Track

Arthur went to Baker Elementary School, where he was an outstanding student. Later he went to Graves Middle School and then to Maggie Walker High School. "Arthur was just the perfect student—quiet and studious," one of his former high school teachers remembered. "He paid attention in class. He didn't chitchat with other students. . . .

But when Arthur did speak, you knew this was an intelligent young man."[6]

Despite his preoccupation with tennis, Arthur managed to be pretty well-rounded, participating in a variety of other activities. In high school he learned to play the trumpet—an early manifestation of his love for music, which would be a sustaining interest throughout his life. And baseball was another passion. He attended a baseball camp during some of his boyhood summers, and for a while Arthur thought he would really do well in high school baseball, but that idea was cut short.

When he was a sophomore, Arthur made the varsity baseball team as a pitcher. In his first outing that year, he pitched one inning and did pretty well. The next day, however, the principal called Arthur into his office and told him he was off the team. This was quite a blow to young Arthur. Being a pitcher on the baseball team carried a lot more prestige with his peers than being a tennis player, even if you were the best.

"Why?" asked the bewildered Arthur.

"Arthur, you've got a great future ahead of you as a tennis player . . . and I don't want to risk you getting hurt," responded the principal.[7]

Arthur later pointed out that this was one of a hundred different occurrences in his life that kept him on track to a tennis career. Talking about the part that luck took in his life, he would comment that "My development was fluke piled upon coincidence."[8]

Racism and Role Models

On Sundays, Arthur went to church and Sunday school. Like the household chores, attending church wasn't something he really wanted to do, especially on a nice summer day, but there was no choice until he left home and could express his own ideas about religion. Even when he was quite young, he became skeptical about the organized church. "I had a scientific mind," he would say, "and there just wasn't any way I could accept the Baptist fundamentalism." It was particularly difficult for Arthur as a black child to look at pictures of the blue-eyed, blond-haired Jesus and feel that this was a deity who was looking out for him. But he never let on to his family, especially Big Mama, that his belief in Jesus was shaken. "I always kept on going to Sunday school and acting in all the church plays," he said.[9]

It wasn't just one church that disappointed Arthur. At various times, he attended the Episcopal, Presbyterian, Baptist, and Roman Catholic churches. He could not accept any of them, but rather, was open to all of them. However, his belief in God and the power of faith and the need for spirituality was unshakable to the end of his life.[10]

As Arthur was growing up, he adopted some role models, mostly men who belonged to minority groups. One of the earliest was Jackie Robinson, who played for the Brooklyn Dodgers in the late 1940s and 1950s. Robinson

A young Arthur Ashe was inspired by Brooklyn Dodger Jackie Robinson, the first African-American player to integrate the major leagues.

was the first African-American player in the major leagues, and practically every black person in the United States became a Dodger fan. Later when Arthur was focusing on tennis, Pancho Gonzalez, a Mexican-American tennis champion, became his idol. Abraham Lincoln was one of his white heroes, because he had freed the slaves. Another, and perhaps his favorite when he was quite young, was Gene Autry, a Hollywood cowboy star his father had taken him to see in a movie when he was six. "Playing cowboys and Indians as a kid, I insisted on being Gene Autry," he later affirmed.[11]

Growing up, Arthur never saw the kind of poverty he would later encounter traveling to the larger cities of the United States on the tennis circuit. Though he lived in a black neighborhood, it was composed of working-class people who lived in decent homes, sent their kids to school, and went to church on Sundays. It was an average American community, except that the people were not allowed in the white communities, unless they were domestic workers of some kind.

"I never saw rat-infested houses, never hung out on corners, never saw anyone knifed," Arthur would say. "We were never poor. Not even close . . ."[12]

Looking out his window, Arthur saw Brook Field spread out before him and thought it was all his. It was almost a dream world for a kid who loved sports. Tennis courts, baseball fields, basketball hoops, a swimming pool—all there at his disposal. Why did he have to go anywhere to look for friends? They all came *here*. "The pool was so full of kids in the summer you couldn't see the water," he later recalled.[13]

So when he was ten and it came time to go to Dr. Johnson's summer tennis camp for two weeks, Arthur's life was full and good. He was hardly aware, in those days, that the society he lived in deprived him of certain rights and benefits because of the color of his skin. Occasionally, however, there were reminders. Like when he got on the bus to Dr. Johnson's camp in Lynchburg. His father took him to the bus station that day, gave him a few last words of advice, put him and his bag and tennis racket on the bus, and waved good-bye.

As the bus pulled away, Arthur saw that the best seat on the bus—for a wide-eyed kid full of wonder—was vacant. It was right near the driver and through the front window there was a clear view of the road and all the scenery ahead. Arthur wiggled into the seat, but he really should have known better. The driver took one look and, without any hostility, said something like "Sorry son, but you can't sit there. You'll have to go to the back." It was an incident Arthur would never forget but for the moment his excitement and eagerness about going to Dr. Johnson's tennis camp offset his disappointment. Only three hours ahead lay Lynchburg: for Arthur it was the promised land.[14]

4

Dr. Johnson's Tennis Boot Camp

When Arthur arrived at Lynchburg, one of Dr. Johnson's assistants picked him up and drove him to the doctor's three-story frame house and expansive grounds on Pierce Street. Immediately he could see the private tennis court amid the lush gardens that were the doctor's pride and joy. Floodlight poles were positioned around the court for playing at night. There was also a garage in the back as well as a children's jungle gym and a dog kennel. Arthur liked dogs but the kennel turned out to be the bane of his existence. Being the youngest in camp, Arthur was assigned the chore of cleaning the kennel, and he never forgot the stench.[1]

Learning at Dr. Johnson's

Arthur was shown his room, one of four upstairs bedrooms, which he would share with another boy. The room had to be straightened up every morning before the boys came down to breakfast. A door from the basement, which served as the locker room, led to the tennis court. Each tennis student had his own place to change clothes, labeled with his name, and two shower stalls were available for the students after practice. The basement also served as a recreation room and included a Ping-Pong table that the boys used to develop timing and coordination. Bookshelves lining the basement were loaded with books and magazines on tennis. "I read them all," Arthur remembered.[2]

Although the tennis facility was not the state-of-the-art type that could be found at an exclusive tennis club, it included all of the necessary training equipment: the Ball Boy machines that endlessly shot balls over the net for trainees to return, a rebounding net, a backboard, and a service device that held the ball at just the right height for practicing serves. Dr. Johnson also had a device that suspended a ball at various heights on an elastic strand. The trainees struck at the ball with a section of broom handle cut the same length as a racket.

The broom-handle technique trained the eye to focus on the ball and develop precision in hitting it. The trainees used the broom handles on the court too, and they practiced until they hit the ball squarely with consistency. New campers could not pick up a real racket until they proved their proficiency with the broom handle.

Arthur looked with wondrous eyes upon Dr. Johnson's well-equipped camp. He could not have imagined that such a place existed. The daily regimen he was expected to follow in tennis training was rigorous, sometimes tedious but mostly enjoyable. He was much less enthusiastic about the chores, which were assigned to all of Dr. Johnson's campers and were enforced. In addition to cleaning the kennel, the students weeded the garden, cut the grass, and maintained the tennis court. Dr. Johnson felt that the chores were a fair compensation for the room and board and tennis training he provided. Arthur understood this, which helped him bear up under the drudgery of manual labor.

At this stage, Arthur's parents shouldered some of his expenses. Indeed, Arthur once overheard his father say that he wished his son had chosen a less expensive sport. Even in those days, a family could spend more than a thousand dollars equipping a serious tennis prospect, and that would be cutting it pretty close to the bone. For Arthur's parents, this was a considerable financial sacrifice, although his parents, with his father working several jobs, were probably better off than most African-American households.[3]

31

Wake-up call at the Johnson camp came around 8:00 A.M. Campers made their own breakfasts, and by 9:00, they were out on the court and hitting balls with one another. They did not play matches very often but concentrated on practicing the various techniques of play. "I believe in practice," Dr. Johnson would say. "You can learn more." Repetition was the key, hitting the same stroke over and over again until it was right: serve, forehand, backhand, crosscourt, overhead, every stroke in the book.[4]

"Dr. Johnson had us hitting crosscourt backhands for forty-five to sixty minutes if you can imagine how boring that was," said Bob Davis, who met Arthur Ashe playing junior ATA tournaments and also spent some summers at the Johnson camp. Davis and Ashe went up the ATA ladder together, playing each other and sometimes teaming as doubles partners. The two remained friends as adults, and eventually Davis established and became president of Black Dynamics, Inc., an organization dedicated to finding a better method of producing top-flight minority tennis players.[5]

Tennis instruction at the camp was provided by Dr. Johnson and his son Robert, known as Bobby. Dr. Johnson had his medical practice, so he was not able to oversee the training all of the time. He trusted the young campers to follow the daily regimen unsupervised, which they did, at least part of the time.

Lunch was served after the morning session, dished out by whoever was available—sometimes Dr. Johnson's secretary and nurse. The afternoon was spent doing drills on the court. When campers were not on the court, they were expected to be working on their chores.

There was no holding back on the food at the Johnson dinner table, which was loaded with a variety of meats and vegetables, along with mounds of rice—Arthur's favorite. Cake, soda pop, ice cream, and most other sweets were not in evidence. Arthur loved mealtime at the Johnson camp. "The meals were one of the reasons I was crazy about the camp from the start," Arthur later wrote.[6]

Despite being skinny as a reed, Arthur loved to eat, and the huge quantities of food he put away astounded everyone. There was no grabbing or greedy gobbling of food at Dr. Johnson's table, however. The rules of etiquette were enforced, and good manners were observed in everyday life situations as well. It was all part of the doctor's plan to eliminate any possible reason for his black players to be rejected because they confirmed white stereotyping. Their behavior on and off the court had to be exemplary, despite the actions of their white counterparts or any mistreatment by white officials.

After dinner the group meandered down to the basement, where Dr. Johnson held a sort of informal classroom session. Instructional films were shown and tennis strategies were discussed. The campers were instructed to read tennis manuals and rule books until they knew them cold, and Dr. Johnson tested them to make sure they did.

Dr. Johnson's Love of Tennis

In his younger days, the doctor was known as "Whirlwind" Johnson, an exceptional athlete who earned Negro All-American honors playing football as a halfback for Lincoln University in Pennsylvania.[7] He was also a superior baseball player and after college he played some semi-pro ball in New York City. He also coached football at several black colleges. Johnson loved sports, but he also knew that his lifework lay elsewhere. He determined that he would take up medicine and enrolled at Meharry Medical College in Nashville. Working his way through school, Johnson had little time for sports, but he realized that he had to do something to stay in shape. He tried various sports, but it wasn't until he hit upon tennis that he settled into a regular mode of exercise. As Dr. Johnson's game improved, he became involved with the ATA and soon was traveling extensively on the ATA tournament circuit.

By the late 1940s, Dr. Johnson was becoming more interested in player development. He had already started

Althea Gibson (left), seen here with Louise Brough, was the
first African-American to break throught the color barrier of the
major tennis tournaments.

working with young players. One of them, who trained
with Dr. Johnson from 1946 to 1951, went on to become the
first African-American player to break through the color
barrier of major U.S. tennis tournaments. Her name was
Althea Gibson. Not only did Dr. Johnson help train the
young Althea, but he became her partner in mixed doubles,
winning seven ATA championships.

Working with the ATA, Dr. Johnson sought out the
finest young black tennis talent. He wanted to develop
players who could reach the highest rungs of championship play.

It wasn't until 1949, however, that his junior development program took its most significant turn. While traveling in June of that year, the doctor found himself in
Charlottesville when the USLTA National Interscholastic

Tennis Tournament was being held on the University of Virginia courts.

Ever the tennis buff, he dropped by to see the action, which featured the best white talent from schools nationwide. Dr. Johnson was impressed with their level of play and realized that most of the players were ahead of the young people he coached. He also realized that the only way his players could reach this level was by competing with the whites. And that meant breaking the color barrier.

Johnson finally approached one of the officials at the tournament and asked if it would be possible to enter some of his players in the next tournament. He was told to apply through the proper channels, which he did, and rather surprisingly, two of his boys were accepted for the 1950 tournament. The boys could not be put up in Charlottesville, like the other entrants, so Dr. Johnson agreed to drive them back and forth the 60 miles (97 km) from Lynchburg.

The tedious drive was short-lived, however, as both of Johnson's boys were trounced in the first round. So soundly were they defeated that an embarrassed Dr. Johnson felt obliged to apologize for their showing. The doctor had already pledged himself to produce top-flight black tennis stars, and this incident forged his resolve into an unremitting determination to achieve that goal. Who knew then that the skinny ten-year-old kid who walked onto his court three years later would fulfill this dream.

Dr. Johnson's Rules

After that first ordeal at the Interscholastics, a deal was struck with the tournament officials. Johnson would hold a tournament each year to determine the best interscholastic black players. The USLTA agreed to hold slots open for the winners. Under this system, Dr. Johnson's players began to make some progress in the previously all-white tournament. His training group was called the junior development team, and he instilled in them ironclad rules of conduct to immunize them against the scrutiny they would be under in the world of white tennis. Their dress, their court manners, and their public interactions, must be impeccable. There would be no disputing calls and, where players made their own line calls, they would always concede to their white opponents.[8]

Bob Davis remembers the court discipline well: "Dr. Johnson had a set of rules that he would not tolerate anybody deviating from. Some of those rules involved the integrity with which we played. A bad call was unheard of. Challenging a bad call was not done. We had balls that were in by a yard called out, and we would walk away. And so when people saw that later on in Arthur—his ability to walk away, to not get excited, to not challenge, to not question—they [didn't] understand that he got as excited as the next guy. We were just conditioned [not to show it]. Dr. Johnson would send us home if we violated any of his rules."[9]

Dr. Johnson's rules were tough and some kids chafed under them and gave up, but for Arthur it was no big deal. "The military-style discipline," Ashe later wrote, "was easy for me to accept because I was accustomed to a similar arrangement in my own house."[10] Indeed Dr. Johnson's and Arthur Sr.'s approaches to life goals were quite similar. Arthur unfailingly praised both men for instilling in him the strength of character he needed to make his way in a virtually all-white sport that was not always receptive and sometimes downright hostile.

5

---------- ⌘ ----------

Advancing in the ATA and USLTA

When Dr. Johnson first saw Arthur play, he did not think the boy had much potential. What changed his mind quickly was Arthur's ability to learn and follow instructions. This capability combined with his dogged determination to do well were what impressed Arthur's instructors. "He was not a pure athlete," Bob Davis would say. "But he compensated for any shortcomings he had by being one of the most disciplined and focused individuals I have ever had the pleasure of meeting."[1]

No Place for a Rebel

Arthur could also be stubbornly loyal, and it was this quality that led to an early crisis at the Dr. Johnson camp—and one that could have short circuited his career. It was within the first few days of Arthur's first summer at the camp that Bobby instructed Arthur to change some of his basic fundamentals of grip and swing. Arthur rebelled immediately. Ron Charity had taught him how to hold the racket and how to swing, and wasn't Ron Charity the greatest? He wouldn't change. He told Bobby that Mr. Charity showed him how to do it the other way, and he would stick to it.

When Bobby reported Arthur's obstinacy to his father, the doctor immediately called Arthur Sr. to come get his son. Within hours, Arthur Sr. stormed into the Johnson complex and sought out his son. He gave it to him straight. Ron Charity had taught him all he could. If he wanted to improve, he had to take instruction from the Johnsons without question. If he wouldn't do that, he could come home that minute. The decision was his. "I stayed. 'Mr. Charity' was never mentioned again in camp," Ashe later wrote.[2]

Arthur was a model of obedience after that. He followed the Johnsons' instructions to a T, no matter what. "He did what you told him, even if he lost at it," Dr. Johnson said. That first summer, Arthur was the youngest, smallest, and spindliest of the players, and he got trounced by everyone in camp.[3] To make up for his size, he tried to build up his stamina, staying on the court longer and practicing harder than anyone else. As a rule, he got up early and got an hour or so on the court before breakfast. This discipline later allowed Arthur to outlast some opponents who were bigger and stronger than he was.[4]

The only real disappointment for Arthur that first summer was not playing in tournaments. Arthur loved the competition of tournament play, but Dr. Johnson felt he was not ready. So even if he was taken along in Dr. Johnson's big Buick, he was only allowed to watch.

Tournament Play

Things got better the next year, when he was eleven, though he was still the smallest kid in camp. In fact, his being there at all had been a bit of an experiment by Dr. Johnson, who previously accepted only teenage players. It would be several years before someone else was the youngest and smallest camper. But in Arthur's second year, Dr. Johnson began to enter him in ATA tournaments, and Arthur won the under-twelve division of every tournament he played in. Dr. Johnson took note.

It was that year too that Arthur found a new idol to worship. Ron Charity, who had been Arthur's idol since he was six, treated Arthur and some other boys to their first professional tennis match. Among the pros Arthur saw that day was Pancho Gonzales, who became Arthur's new hero. Arthur admired Gonzales because of his power game and because, he, like Arthur, also belonged to an ethnic minority.[5]

The next summer, his third with Dr. Johnson, Arthur entered the under-thirteen division of the ATA national championships at Durham, North Carolina. He won all his preliminary matches and went into the finals, which he also won. It was the first of eleven national ATA titles that Arthur Ashe would win from 1955 to 1962.

Now the local tennis world was beginning to take note of Arthur, the skinny little kid from Richmond who was beating about everybody in the boy's division, no matter their size. Even the stern Dr. Johnson was impressed with his young protégé. He began to enter Arthur in matches with juniors and adult men, just to see what he could do. He usually lost, but Arthur was now a dominant player in his own age group.

In his fourth summer with Dr. Johnson, Arthur turned thirteen, and he experienced the onset of puberty with its accompanying growth spurt and the complications of adolescence. Dr. Johnson by then felt his experiment with Arthur was quite a success and began to bring in younger kids. This reduced the pressure on Arthur, who was no longer the smallest kid in the camp. He graduated to better chores and saw an end to the teasing he took because of his size. Arthur had now become one of the seasoned "pros" of the camp. As such, he was one of a select few, a result of the considerable attrition rate at the camp. Dr. Johnson was focused on finding the most promising black tennis players, and those who did not do well in tournaments were quickly replaced. Arthur was never replaced.

A Maturing Player

In 1958, when Arthur was fifteen, Dr. Johnson thought he was "ready." He felt Arthur had reached a skill level and was psychologically prepared to enter major USLTA tournaments against white competition. The year before, he had won the ATA National Championship for the under-fifteen division and played in his first mixed tournament, reaching the semifinals before losing. When Arthur was still fourteen, he and another camper, Tom Hawes, had fought their way into the final game of the Middle States Clay Court Junior Championships. Tom, who was older, defeated Arthur in the final match, becoming the first black youth to win in a white tournament. When Arthur went back to his middle school that fall, he was entered in the Virginia High School Championships, which he won, although he was sometimes matched against opponents three years older than himself.

Dr. Johnson wanted to see how Arthur would do against top-level white competition. However, the problem was not so much whether Arthur was ready to play at the next level, but whether or not he would be allowed to play in major USLTA tournaments, where black participation was limited. And he had to compete in those tournaments in order to improve his game.

Some of the tournaments, mostly those held outside the South, did accept him. But the one Arthur most wanted to play in was the Mid-Atlantic Championships, held that year in Richmond at the Country Club of Virginia. It was Arthur's hometown, and he wanted to play for his friends and neighbors, but his application was turned down. Race could be the only reason for the refusal—even the USLTA ranked Arthur fifth nationally in his age group that year.

That summer, Arthur reached the semifinals in the New Jersey Boys Tournament and won the state championship in the Maryland Junior Tournament. Also there were two significant "firsts" for Arthur that year: it was the first year he made it into the National Boys Championships at Kalamazoo, and in an ATA tournament, he beat his mentor Ron Charity for the first time.

Arthur's game also began to take on a new dimension when he was fifteen. The year marked the first semblance of his development as a power player, although it would be some years before Arthur would perfect this style. Previously, Dr. Johnson had emphasized a strong ground-

40

stroke game, staying back at the baseline and returning the ball on the bounce. Now he could at times rush the net and volley, ripping the ball on the fly back to his opponent's court. Dr. Johnson also emphasized the backhand stroke, theorizing that most opponents hit to the backhand because most players are weakest with that stroke. As a result, Arthur's backhand became his best weapon, and one that became the undoing of many an unwary opponent. The backhand combined with Arthur's serve, which he now delivered with power and accuracy, became the cornerstone of Arthur's game.

Arthur's tennis playing now extended beyond Dr. Johnson's camp. Having graduated from Graves Middle School, he entered Maggie Walker High School in the fall of 1958 and was immediately grabbed up by the tennis team. Maggie Walker, like Arthur's previous schools, was all black. Integration had not yet reached Richmond. The tennis team was not a distinguished group, except for Arthur. In his sophomore and junior years, Arthur won the black High School State Tournament.[6]

A Little Romance

The first stirring of romance came to Arthur, then in his sophomore year and attracting the young ladies of Maggie Walker. Arthur still had to follow his father's strict disciplinary code, however, which tended to put something of a damper on his social life. He had to be home by eleven o' clock, which the other kids thought was really old-fashioned. Once, when he didn't come home from a party by curfew, Arthur Sr. showed up to get him. When Mr. Ashe walked in, one of the girls commented, "Hey, Art, here is your antique father."[7]

Arthur grew up in a black world, and through high school he dated only black girls. His first encounter with white girls was at the USLTA tournaments, but these were passing acquaintances. One enduring romance did spring up through an ATA tournament, however. Arthur was still fifteen when he met Pat Battles, whose father was a black

41

teaching pro. She was a stunning young lady with long, wavy hair, and Arthur was knocked out from almost the first moment. The relationship might have developed faster, but distance was a problem. The Battles lived in Stamford, Connecticut, far from Richmond, so the two saw one another mainly during summer tournaments. Nevertheless, Arthur and Pat became devoted to one another and remained sweethearts for years.[8]

As a Teenager

Arthur's tennis reputation continued to grow through his sixteenth year, his seventh with Dr. Johnson. Early in 1959, Arthur and another of Dr. Johnson's players, Horace Cunningham, were the first blacks to be invited to a major USLTA tournament in the South, the Orange Bowl International Junior Cup with player-representatives from fifteen nations. Arthur was thrilled. He loved to travel and enjoyed the distinction of playing in the tournament, but there was also the remote possibility of being chosen for a Junior Davis Cup team that would represent the United States in a tournament.

Even if he won the tournament, however, Arthur knew his chances of being chosen were slim in this Southern city. No African-American had ever made the team. Arthur played well, nevertheless, winning his first four matches before falling to a more highly skilled and better trained player from Puerto Rico. It was a fateful meeting between the two. Arthur encountered that adversary many more times in juniors and as an adult, and their lives were to become closely intertwined. The boy's name was Charlie Pasarell.

With summer Arthur turned sixteen and was back at Dr. Johnson's camp. Now he was entering the junior division, which then extended to eighteen-year-olds. Play was tougher now against older and more experienced competition. But, no matter, Arthur was used to playing the older boys. One his most memorable junior matches that year came in the New Jersey State Tournament finals when he was pitted against Herb FitzGibbon, who had demolished him at Kalamazoo the previous year. This time Arthur used a new strategy devised by Dr. Johnson.

His opponent was a 6-foot (183-centimeter) powerhouse net rusher. Arthur won his early matches with smashing passing shots, but Dr. Johnson did not think this would work on FitzGibbon. Instead he had Arthur drive the opponent back from the net with deep lobs. Arthur lost the first two sets, 6–1, 6–1, but he stuck to his game plan. FitzGibbon began to wear out in the third set, and Arthur got the signal to start slamming his passing shots past his exhausted foe. Arthur took the last three sets, 7–5, 6–1, 6–0. Dr. Johnson's strategy had worked, but it took Arthur's great conditioning and discipline to carry it off.

Arthur's application for the Mid-Atlantic Tournament was again turned down in 1959, with the obviously false statement that it had arrived too late. Arthur knew of white players, less qualified than he, who applied later and got in. He was now ranked forty-fourth overall in the nation by the USLTA, but the Mid-Atlantic didn't rate him at all because it would not let him play. The rejection saddened Arthur, and he began to wonder whether he could ever get anywhere in tennis if he could not play the top players in his home region. He fought off his despair with the help of Dr. Johnson and his father. Dr. Johnson knew that Arthur could develop into a national star, but only if he could play against top competition year-round. Dr. Johnson had a plan, but Arthur had to finish his junior year before it could be implemented.

Arthur only got to the third round at the Boys' Championships at Kalamazoo, but because he was one of the two top juniors in ATA, he was allowed to enter the national tournament for amateurs at Forest Hills in New York City. He was beaten in the first round that year by twenty-one-year-old Rod Laver. Laver played in the finals the next three years, winning in 1962, and went on to become one of the all-time tennis greats.

In 1959, Arthur lost at Forest Hills to Rod Laver, who went on to be one of the all-time greats. Laver is shown here with the 1962 U.S. Championship trophy.

Arthur returned to high school in Richmond for his junior year. He had an excellent year academically and enjoyed a fairly active social life. He was now able to borrow the family car for dates and parties, which was a rite of passage for him, as it is for most teenagers. Some fairly "serious" romantic relationships developed despite his long-distance romance with Pat Battles.

Through it all, Arthur's mind remained firmly locked on tennis. In Richmond he did not have a lot of opportunity to play in winter but did well when invited to meets in the warmer climes. In June 1960, he entered the USLTA National Interscholastics. Winning that tournament had been the driving force behind Dr. Johnson's junior development program. This year, Arthur worked his way into the quarterfinals and faced Bill Lenoir, an Atlanta boy who was a favorite to win the tournament.

The match started well for Arthur as he put away the first set and went ahead 4–3 in the second. Arthur won the next point but a stray ball rolled onto the court at the moment Lenoir was lunging at Arthur's return. Arthur, trained to obey the rules to the letter and to concede close calls to his opponent, asked Lenoir if the ball had distracted him. Whether it did or not, Lenoir grabbed the opportunity to replay the point, which he won. The incident unnerved Arthur despite his conditioning to be nonreactive, and Lenoir went on to win the match and the tournament. Once again, the rare prize of winning the Interscholastics had eluded Dr. Johnson.

At Seventeen

A few weeks later in the early summer of 1960, Arthur Ashe turned seventeen. He had by now just about reached his full height of 6 feet (183 cm). Weighing perhaps less than 150 pounds (68 kilograms), he was still reed thin, which may have lulled some opponents into thinking he wasn't a threat. But the years of conditioning had developed a lithe muscular network that stretched over his long, narrow frame, and his power game grew accordingly. Blessed with

45

superb coordination and timing, Arthur moved across the court with an uncommon grace that observers would see as "poetry in motion."

Arthur was back at Dr. Johnson's camp that summer for training and more tournament play. As he had been almost every year since joining with Dr. Johnson, Arthur was entered into the ATA championship tournaments. His performance in the ATA matches that year became his crowning achievement to date. First he was entered in the Junior Negro Championship, which he won, beating his own thirteen-year-old brother, John, along the way. John was now also considered a tennis prodigy. After wrapping up the junior championship, Arthur was entered into the men's Senior Negro Championship, in which he had played before but not won. That year he claimed the Men's Championship, becoming the youngest player ever to win the men's division and the first to sweep the junior and senior crowns in a single year. Arthur Ashe, Jr., at seventeen, was now unequivocally the best black tennis player in the United States, and probably the world. There were still many white mountains to climb out there, but people, important people, were watching, and plans were being laid.[9]

6

Slamming in St. Louis

For seventeen-year-old Arthur Ashe, 1960 was a very good year. Along with his ATA triumphs, Arthur settled a long simmering aspiration to play in the Mid-Atlantic Sectional, the tournament that had barred him when it was held in his hometown of Richmond. It was different this year though. The matches were held in Wheeling, West Virginia, and Arthur was admitted. He did not disappoint, beating the number-one sectional player for the championship. He may have been the first black male to win a USLTA tournament at that level.[1]

His performance in the USLTA juniors at Kalamazoo improved considerably in 1960, with upsets of two highly graded players, a Rhodesian youth in the second round and a Junior Davis Cup team member in the third. With only an hour's rest, Arthur had to come back and play his fourth-round match against a tough opponent in sweltering 92°F (33°C) heat. Even with his superb conditioning, Arthur could not rebound. With a few hours to recoup his strength, he might have gone to the finals, but instead he lost and was out of the tournament. Of course, he did not complain of the unfairness of the situation; he had been trained for years to accept whatever happened without a whimper, especially in white tournaments.

Playing Tennis in a Segregated World

Even so, his accomplishments that summer at Kalamazoo were highly encouraging and his reputation continued to grow, drawing national attention. Even Arthur did not realize then that people who were to catapult his career were already taking note. It was pretty well acknowledged now by Dr. Johnson and others that Arthur could enter the top national rankings in tennis if he continued to improve. To do that, he had to be able to play year-round the way the California players did. Arthur had noticed how advanced the California players were at Kalamazoo—they seemed almost another breed. Segregated Richmond was not the place to progress. There he was barred from the best indoor facilities and could not play against the best competitors, anyway, because they were white.[2]

Despite his success in tennis, the specter of race continued to follow Arthur as he played the ATA and USLTA circuits. It was not just being barred from playing in tournaments held at whites-only clubs, but the constant difficulty of finding a place to stay, place to eat, and admission to public places. Expenses were also a problem. Accommodations generally came through a network of black families who put the players up whenever they were in their community. "We would call and say he's coming . . . can you keep him?" said Virginia Glass. "There was a tremendous amount of family feeling and reciprocity among members of the ATA."[3] Glass came to know Arthur well from the days her sons, Luis and Sydney, trained with him at the Johnson camp. When Arthur came to New York during his teen years to play Forest Hills, he often stayed with the Glasses, then residents of the city.

Dr. Johnson usually drove his players to tournaments in his Buick. It was a large car but the kids were sometimes crowded together, and the drive could take many hours. Virginia Glass recalls her sons' reactions: "Invariably my sons . . . would call me and complain, 'There are too many in the car,' and 'I can't stand living in this room with four people,' and I would say, 'Talk to Art,' because Art had a calming influence on them."

Sometimes housing would be arranged but be withdrawn when it was learned that the children were black. This happened to the Glass kids in Delaware. "I had to enlist the aid of Marian Anderson [the late Metropolitan Opera contralto]," Glass said. "She got housing for them at the YMCA." Glass dropped the boys off there, telling them they were only restricted from using the pool. "But you know how kids are. When I got back, they had won both events and they said, 'We had a great time in the pool—every time we got in, everybody got out.' "[4]

The experiences of trying to break into white tennis always stayed with Arthur. Sydney Glass was on the circuit with Arthur. He remembered that "there were no black kids playing in any [USLTA] tournaments at all. Basically, every time we played in a 'white tournament,' it was not just a tennis match; it was also a sort of a minor civil rights struggle going on a lot of the time . . . all the white kids could act like total brats and we always had to act perfectly. Dr. Johnson basically said, '[Y]ou're here representing the American Tennis Association, you're representing Negroes (sic).' . . . Arthur from the time he was fourteen was pretty amazing at times [at] just being able to cope. He was so good so soon that he was always the one black person who was sent here and there and he was afforded a number of opportunities and with those opportunities came a price. You know, he had to really act as the consummate sportsman. . . . Arthur, since he was a kid, was an ambassador."[5]

Bob Davis too recalls his experience traveling the segregated South with Arthur. "I remember one particular incident in which Arthur and I were staying in a YMCA, and in the middle of the night somebody put a fire ax right through . . . our door. And truly the message was to go away. But we stayed. Tennis did not embrace us."[6]

When Arthur was playing the USLTA junior circuit, he often found himself isolated as the lone black entered in a tournament. Socialization was difficult, especially in the South, and enduring it took all the inner strength that his father and Dr. Johnson had instilled in him. But there were moments of gratification as well. During the 1960 National Interscholastics in Charlottesville, for instance, three of the top players—Butch Newman, Cliff Buchholz, and Charlie Pasarell—all white, asked Arthur to accompany them to a movie. Arthur was reluctant, knowing that the movie house was probably restricted. The boys insisted, however, and Arthur agreed without too much difficulty, because he really did want to go. When they got to the theater, the scene was just what Arthur had dreaded. He would not be admitted. Arthur was hardened to segregation but still could feel somewhat downcast. His spirits were lifted, however, when Cliff Buchholz piped up, "Well, if he can't go in, none of us will go." And the four trekked off together. Such displays of comradeship helped keep Arthur on track to achieve his tennis goals.[7]

Off to St. Louis

Unbeknownst to Arthur, over the summer, plans had been made that would significantly change his life. They were made on the premise that Arthur had to play tennis year-round to reach his potential, and that could not happen in Richmond. Dr. Johnson, with Arthur Sr.'s consent, had made contact with Richard Hudlin of St. Louis, Missouri, who agreed to take over the reins that would guide Arthur into his tennis future. It was decided that Arthur should live with Hudlins in St. Louis for his senior year and attend Sumner High School, where Mr. Hudlin was a teacher. Of course Arthur had to agree to all this. It meant uprooting, leaving his home, his family, and his friends. It meant leaving high school in his senior year and going from all that was familiar to a strange and unknown world. Not a prospect that would appeal to most kids.

But Arthur was not just any kid, not by a long shot. He would miss the familiar surroundings of Richmond. And not graduating with his class was painful to contemplate. But Arthur knew what was at stake. As he said in *Advantage Ashe*, "Even if there hadn't been the color barrier

His senior high school year in St. Louis was good for Arthur, shown here winning the 1961 National Interscholastic Tennis Championship.

onship, and it was also the most satisfying moment in his young tennis career.

It did not stop there, however. Arthur looked back upon 1960–1961 in St. Louis as a great year in tennis and in scholastics. He ended his senior year at Sumner with the highest grade point average in his class and would have been valedictorian except for a residency requirement. Socially, he was under tight restrictions, as he had been at home, but in tennis it was all upbeat.

After High School

In May 1961, Arthur was entered once again in the USLTA Interscholastic Tournament at Charlottesville, the event Dr. Johnson had dreamed of winning with a black champion ever since he started his tennis camp. This year, Dr.

Johnson's dream was fulfilled. Arthur roared through the tournament, blowing away the opposition without losing a set. It was his second national title, and Arthur could now foresee himself a major force in tennis.

There was more that summer of 1961. Arthur won his second ATA men's singles title and, for an extra thrill, won the men's doubles, teaming up with his first mentor, Ron Charity. This gave Charity his only ATA championship, and Arthur was deeply gratified for that. He also fought his way into the semifinals at Kalamazoo but was taken out in an upset by his old friend from St. Louis, Cliff Buchholz. It was an unfortunate loss because it could have been Arthur's third national championship that season and a certain number-one junior national ranking. As it was, he was rated fifth, with first place going to good chum Charlie Pasarell.

Despite the ranking, Arthur caught the eye of Tom Price, the man who almost arbitrarily selected the Junior Davis Cup team. Price offered a spot on the team to Arthur, who was thrilled and proud. It was a huge honor and the fulfillment of another dream for Arthur. Being on the team placed Arthur in the most select group of young tennis players nationally, virtually assuring his future in tennis.[13]

Tom Price was not the only one to notice Arthur's rise. Someone else who would play a most significant role in Arthur's immediate future had been watching the young tennis star for a couple of years. By the fall of 1960, he had written to Arthur. The letter Arthur received at that time was from J. D. Morgan, the tennis coach at the University of California/Los Angeles (UCLA) and director of one of the top college tennis programs in the United States. The coach suggested that Arthur might pursue his tennis career at that university. Arthur could think about it. On the way back from the Orange Bowl Tournament at Christmastime, Arthur stopped off to see his family in Richmond. Shortly after he arrived a phone call came from Morgan. The coach offered Arthur a full scholarship to come and play tennis at UCLA, the first ever offered by that school to an African-American.

Arthur's good friend Charlie Pasarell

Arthur did not hesitate. He knew UCLA's ranking as a tennis school, and he snapped up the offer. Arthur was a particularly attractive choice because, in addition to his tennis skills, he had a superior scholastic record, bordering on almost straight-A's through high school. Other schools, including Harvard, Hampton Institute, Michigan, Michigan State, and Arizona, had also made offers, but UCLA was the one Arthur had been hoping for. Only the University of Southern California University (USC) rivaled UCLA in tennis in those years.[14]

At the end of the summer of 1961, Arthur, now a fully developed eighteen-year-old, packed his bags one more time and headed for the coast, college, and tennis fame.

7

———— ∾ ————

College Life and Intercollegiate Tennis

When Arthur Ashe arrived on the UCLA campus, he was set to embark upon the highest realm of intercollegiate tennis. It was a time when virtually all of the top U.S. tennis stars came out of the college ranks. Within a generation, top-flight players were skipping the college circuit and heading right into major tournaments. Jimmy Connors and John McEnroe, not many years after Ashe's college days, played one year at UCLA and Stanford respectively before moving on. This exodus was brought on primarily by the advent of open tennis in 1968 and the flight into professional tennis with its lure of ever-increasing purse sizes. But in 1961, the players who stocked the Davis Cup teams and played for the biggest prizes were at schools such as UCLA, USC, Stanford, and others, mostly in the West, South, and Southwest.[1]

From the time Ashe won his first national USTA tournament, he was the first black male to achieve each new accomplishment in tennis. Frequently Ashe has been compared to Jackie Robinson, who broke through the color barrier in major-league baseball. The main difference was that Robinson was chosen from a large pool of highly qualified players in the black baseball leagues. After Robinson opened the gate, a flood of quality black players poured into the majors. Nothing similar happened with Ashe in tennis. Whereas Robinson soon had lots of company, Ashe remained the lone black male playing at the top level of tennis. And little changed in that regard in the decades that followed.[2]

Life at UCLA

What a strange and wondrous new world the UCLA campus was. For the first time in his life, Ashe was living on his own in an integrated society. This is not to say that Ashe did not encounter incidents of racism on the campus and in the Los Angeles area. Though it was an integrated campus, there was still plenty of prejudice to go around. It smacked him right in the face almost from his first moments on campus. One of the regular invitational tournaments that UCLA team members played was at a place called the Balboa Bay Club. J. D. Morgan told Ashe the usual invitations had been extended, but he had been excluded. The coach asked if he wanted to make an issue of it and said he would stick with Ashe on any decision he made, even cancel the date for the other UCLA players.[3]

Shades of Richmond and Charlottesville! Here he had barely arrived on campus and already there was a crisis. But this was nothing new for Ashe. He was used to this sort of thing; the rejection just surprised him a little here in multicultural Los Angeles. Ashe could have made an official protest, but he kept a cool head. He was already known nationally in tennis circles, and he guessed that his reputation would continue to grow. There would come a time when he would have lots of leverage and would be able to call the shots in this kind of situation. That time had not yet come, but it was not far off. Starting off in controversy was not wise. Ashe knew it and so did Morgan, who agreed with Ashe's decision not to protest. From the beginning, Ashe trusted Morgan and had faith in his direction.

On October 29 of that first year, three members of the UCLA squad did play in the invitational, including

The 1962 NCAA Championship team from UCLA (left to right):
Ian Crookenden, Dave Sanderlin, Coach J. D. Morgan,
Dave Reed, and Arthur Ashe

Charlie Pasarell, the kid from Puerto Rico who had
played many junior tournaments with Ashe, who had
also decided on UCLA.[4] Later, when Ashe was the sixth-
ranked U.S. player and a member of the Davis Cup team,
the same club invited him to their tournament. Ashe de-
clined and continued to decline in succeeding years.

Ashe had been under the control of one mentor or another all his life. Until he went to college, virtually every
waking moment was planned out for him. He did experience some freedom when he went to tournaments on his
own, but somebody was always watching. Morgan continued that control in tennis at UCLA, but off the court Ashe
was now his own man. He made his own decisions and did
not have to answer to anyone. Later he would say, however,
that even in his late twenties and thirties, when he did

something wrong he had the feeling that somehow his father would show up and set him straight.[5]

College life was fascinating for Ashe. The era of coed dorms had begun, and Ashe went to live at Sproul Hall, a massive housing unit with a broad mix of students, male and female. Sam Beale, a Jewish student, was the first of a string of white roommates that Ashe had in college. The first girl he dated in college was an American-born Japanese girl, Susan Ikei. It was his first date with a girl who was not African-American, and it was also her first date with a black American. The two became very close and developed a kinship based on their mutual experiences with racial prejudice. Susan's parents has been forced into internment camps during World War II. The Japanese were also often excluded from private clubs, so she could sympathize with Ashe's Balboa Bay Club experience.

The campus also gave Ashe his first real encounter with foreign students, many of whom wore the traditional clothing of their homelands in Asia or Africa. He enjoyed the exchange of views with people whose backgrounds were so different from his own. This also led to some political wrangling on campus. Black militancy was on the rise in the early 1960s, and black groups wanted for all African-American men to step forward and be counted, especially those who had gained some celebrity. Ashe at this juncture in his life resisted "getting involved" to a large degree. He did join a black fraternity, Kappa Alpha Psi, when he had his choice of many that would accept him. But for the most part, tennis and studies were all-absorbing.

The pressure to do more for causes, black and otherwise, would pursue Ashe for much of his life. He did do more in time, but looking back on that period, Ashe would say in his writings, "You can't be [number one] on a tennis court and spend all your time in the black community. Muhammad Ali didn't do it, Martin Luther King didn't do it. . . . If I had the luxury of being able to devote all my time to tennis, instead of being diverted every once in a while into black causes . . . I would have been a better player."[6]

College Academics

Ashe enjoyed studying and learning. It had always come to him easily, but he did have to go into a remedial English course in his first year. This came as a bit of a shock because Ashe had always enjoyed writing, and his high school teachers gave him high praise for his essays. But apparently college demands were tougher and some of his writing mechanics had to be fine-tuned.[7]

Ashe's first academic inclination at UCLA was to go for architecture. He was bright enough to do well in either, he thought. Morgan, however, was quick to point out that tennis was going to occupy a lot of Ashe's time, and architecture would require intensive study on a daily basis. The coach suggested business school would make more sense. Ashe trusted Morgan and could see his point. He chose business administration, and it was a decision he never regretted. Using the skills he learned in college later helped him deal with his own rather complicated finances and considerable business involvement.[8]

Ashe did well in business school, but not as well as he might have done if tennis did not occupy so much of his time. He was away a lot at tournaments, and there was practice every afternoon. Fortunately, the tennis courts were right outside of Sproul Hall, but sometimes the pace was too much and he fell behind in his class work. When that happened, Morgan arranged for a tutor, a fairly common occurrence for scholarship athletes. Arthur felt the tutor was a great time saver. "A tutor can teach you more in two hours than a professor gives the class in a week," Ashe would say. The money to pay for tutors was usually donated by alumni.[9] But by and large, his classes were a snap.

Outside of Class

Also like other athletes, Arthur was given a part-time job so that he could earn some spending money. He was mainly assigned to maintaining the tennis courts, a familiar task since he did the same thing for Dr. Johnson. The pay was

$2.50 an hour and he was required to put in some 250 hours over the school year.[10]

There was another breakthrough for Ashe during his freshman year. He had his first date with a white girl. This may not seem particularly noteworthy in today's society, but for a black kid from the South in the early 1960s, it was quite a different story. In Ashe's hometown a black man could get beat up, or worse, for trying to socialize with a white girl. He knew in his mind that it was unlikely to cause any furor at UCLA, but it still took considerable courage to overcome the taboos of the South and walk across a dance floor to ask an attractive brunette to dance. It was his first dance with a white girl, and their meeting spawned a relationship.

Everything went well until the girl's mother saw a picture of Ashe on television and realized that the tennis player her daughter had been talking about was black. She then gave her daughter some stern advice. That hampered the relationship, but it continued for some months anyway, finally cooling of its own accord. From the experience, Ashe concluded that "women were women and they were all different."

Having gotten past the "white mystique," Ashe began dating women of different races, and he enjoyed mixing with women of different ethnic and cultural backgrounds. Ashe also found out something else very quickly. At UCLA, as a top athlete, he enjoyed celebrity status.[11] Add to that his good looks, intelligence, and the exotic appeal of being black, and even the somewhat shy, laid-back Ashe had no trouble dating.

On the Court at UCLA

Ashe won most of his matches as a freshman, though he was not invincible. Nevertheless, Ashe's game kept getting better with Morgan's motivational coaching. Morgan stayed on top of Ashe and wouldn't let him slack off in his practice or in matches. Ashe was a highly self-disciplined person, but he occasionally let his mind wander during play. Morgan had his ways of snapping Ashe back to reality, however. Anytime Ashe let up or seemed to be daydreaming, Morgan told him off in front his peers, and the threat of that embarrassment generally kept Ashe focused.[12]

Morgan also brought in some of the top pros of the area to hit with the squad, and Ashe felt his game improved markedly from the experience. Among the pros were Pancho Gonzalez, Ashe's childhood idol, Pancho Seguera, and Alex Olmedo. J. D.'s methods must have worked because UCLA was always in the running for the intercollegiate crown. His winning drive was so contagious that in Ashe's third year, the school appointed Morgan athletic director. He continued to coach tennis for a few more years though, before taking up his new position full-time. During Morgan's years as athletic director, UCLA underwent a golden era in sports.

Ashe's childhood idol and eventual opponent, Pancho Gonzalez

A UCLA team of any kind could have a great year, but a loss to arch crosstown rival USC could put a damper on the whole season. That's how fierce the rivalry was between the two schools. And USC was really tough while Ashe was at UCLA, especially the first three years. Among the USC players were Dennis Ralston, Rafael Osuna, Tom Edlefsen, Ramsey Earnhardt, and Bill Bond. Bob Lutz and Stan Smith came along near the end of Ashe's college reign. All became highly ranked players.

Especially menacing for Ashe was Ralston, who was a year ahead. He usually beat Ashe in college and thereafter. For Ashe, Ralston was the barrier that stood between him and the intercollegiate singles championship. At the end of Ashe's freshman year in 1962, it was USC that won the national intercollegiate championship, leaving a pall of gloom over the UCLA courts. UCLA had been dominant in college tennis for several years previously.

Ashe was not quite up to the speed of some of the best incoming freshman players. He had received probably the best training a black tennis player could get in his time, but it could not compare with that of the white players, who had access to the best clubs and the best coaching and who had played against the best competition since childhood. For Ashe it had always been an uphill battle to play with the top players. During his last year at St. Louis, he had overcome that problem to a large extent. He was the fifth-ranked junior in the nation when he came to UCLA, as well as the number-one player in the Middle Atlantic region and number-one in the ATA. No question he had the temperament, the conditioning, and the talent to be a winner, but his skills still needed some sharpening.

By the time the 1961 national rankings came out, freshman Ashe was ranked twenty-ninth in the U.S. men's division, just behind Charlie Pasarell. Most of the players up at the top of the heap were a year or more ahead of Ashe. They included Chuck McKinley, Donald Dell, Frank Froehling, Allen Fox, Billy Bond, Dennis Ralston, Larry Nagler, Billy Lenoir, and Marty Riessen. At the National Hardcourt

Tournament at La Jolla, California, in December 1962, shortly before the rankings came out, Ashe was up against a tough field but made it into the third round of play. Then he was matched against the number-eight player, teammate Allen Fox, the 1961 intercollegiate champion, who won in straight sets. Pasarell made it into the quarterfinals before also losing to Fox, but Billy Lenoir never made it out of the first round. Fox was the eventual tournament winner, so Ashe had had the misfortune to draw a hot player in an early round.

As the year wore on, Ashe's skills continued to sharpen under the tutelage of Morgan and Gonzales. By spring, the freshman felt ready to challenge anybody. One of the big West Coast tournaments is held each year at Ojai Valley, California, and traditionally it attracts some of the best players in the West. In the men's singles, Arthur blew through the early rounds without losing a set and found himself in the semifinals. His opponent in the semis turned out to be Charlie Pasarell. Now Ashe's improving game was just about equal to Pasarell's. The two buddies squared off in a hard-fought match. When the smoke cleared, Ashe was the victor, 6–3, 3–6, 6–2. The final match was against Dave Reed, who would become Ashe's sophomore roommate. Ashe put Reed away, 6–3, 6–2. He had dropped only one set in the tournament.

On the Circuit

At the next National Hardcourt Tournament in Seattle, Washington, in June, Ashe made it into the quarterfinals before losing to UCLA team captain Larry Nagler. A few weeks later, Ashe was at the National Clay Court Tournament in Chicago, Illinois. School was out now and Ashe was on the summer circuit. He no longer had to struggle to get into these tournaments. Now he had a national reputation and was invited, usually with transportation and living expenses picked up by the tourney sponsors.

Clay is slow and this was no longer Ashe's game. He was used to the fast California hard courts and the power game they encouraged. Nevertheless, Ashe made a respectable showing in Chicago, eliminating Chris Crawford, Keith Carpenter, and USC's promising Tom Edlefsen, before going down in the quarterfinals to Australian Fred Stolle, 8–6, 6–1. Stolle lost in the finals to Chuck McKinley. Later that summer, Ashe played in the Pennsylvania Grass Court Tournament. In the singles, he lost to Clark Graebner of Northwestern University in an early round, but teamed up with Nagler and went to the top in doubles.

At the end of that summer, Ashe entered the U.S. National Championships, held then at Forest Hills, New York. Having seen his game continually improve through the summer, Arthur went into the tournament with confidence. But the U.S. National Championships was not at all like the regional and local tournaments he had been playing. Forest Hills was a grand slam event, one of the four major international tournaments held each year. The field at these matches continues to be huge, and they attract the world's top-seeded players. Arthur did well in the first round, but in the second the draw went against him. He found himself facing off against Roy Emerson of Australia, one of the world's great players and a top seed in the tournament. Emerson, who had won the championship at Forest Hills the previous year, would in his career win twenty-eight grand slam tournaments, an all-time record. Ashe was overmatched, but he gave a good account of himself before succumbing, 6–2, 6–3, 6–0.[13]

As his sophomore year at UCLA approached, Arthur could look back with satisfaction on the strides he had made as a freshman. He eagerly awaited the still greater challenges ahead.

8

For School
and Country

After Forest Hills 1962, it was back to the books and the intercollegiate circuit for sophomore Ashe. He was again living at Sproul Hall, but this time his roommate was David Reed, also a member of the UCLA tennis squad. The accommodations this year were also more posh, reflecting the school's recognition of the two tennis stars. Ashe's off-the-court life continued on an even keel, and his social life improved as he shook off his freshman insecurities.

Ashe liked to play the field socially, enjoying the variety of dates available on campus. In the background though was his relationship with Pat Battles, the girl he had been seeing off and on since his ATA tournament days, and for whom he continued to have strong feelings.

He remained in close touch with his father and kept up his Richmond connections and his ties with Dr. Johnson. However, ever since St. Louis, Ashe's time in Virginia was limited. Even before that, during his Maggie Walker days, he was away much of the summer as his game developed and tournament demands increased. He never again actually lived in Richmond, nor did he have any desire to return to the city whose white tennis society had rejected him. One day Richmond would apologize for the past and honor its native son.

Ashe clung to the values that he grew up with, but his physical image had undergone some changes. He remained long and lean, but he had adopted a new hairstyle popular among athletes of the period. It was called a "flattop" cut, a kind of a crew cut with a flat inclined surface. Another change was precipitated during a drive to Tijuana, Mexico, after a tournament in La Jolla. Pasarell read a sign aloud: "Tijuana 17 miles." Ashe could see the sign but could not make out the lettering, and for the first time he realized that his sight was less than perfect. Soon thereafter he was wearing the dark horn-rimmed frames that became a kind of trademark of the early Ashe. And what a thrill it was to see things clearly for the first time. "I never realized that I had been living in a blur," Arthur later commented.[1]

A New Season

UCLA entered the 1962–1963 intercollegiate season with a forbidding lineup of tennis talent, headed by a powerful sophomore contingent, including Arthur Ashe and Charlie Pasarell. Rounding out the team were Bruce Campbell, Thorvald Moe, Paul Palmer, David Reed, and David Sanderlin. They could feel good about having a dominant team for years to come. The only problem was that USC also had an all-star team. It was headed by Rafael Osuna and Dennis Ralston, two of the best U.S. players, both ranked above any of the UCLA players. The intercollegiate championships in the spring of 1963 were head-to-head battles between the two schools. But the juggernaut combo of Osuna-Ralston was unbeatable. That year USC lost to no one in conference play, and UCLA lost only to USC.

Ashe played well throughout the season, which included a championship victory in the Southern California Intercollegiates that was highlighted by a stunning defeat of Ralston in a semifinal match. He also garnered victories over Osuna and the University of California's highly regarded Jim McManus. In the Athletic Association of Western Universities (AAWU) conference play, Ashe fought his way into the finals, where he challenged Ralston and lost.

Clearly, Ralston would be Ashe's nemesis until he graduated from college a year ahead of Ashe. In the USC–UCLA dual meets that year, Ashe did not fare so well, losing to both

Osuna and Ralston. The toughness of the competition was reflected in the schools' lineups, which included three winners of the Davis Cup and seven nationally ranked players.[2]

In 1962, Ashe had been ranked eighteenth nationally, and by the end of his sophomore year he was UCLA's number-one gun. Now even bigger things were in the offing. During his sophomore year, Arthur had been invited to many tournaments. He could not attend all of them because of school commitments. But his reputation was well known now, and when he went to tournaments, he was an honored guest. He had played one grand slam tournament, at Forest Hills, and longed to play in the other three. One of these was coming up at the end of the school year. It was the pinnacle of world tournament play: Wimbledon. For most tennis players, entering this All-England tournament was the equivalent of reaching Nirvana. All of the top-ranked U.S. players would be attending, including Pasarell, Ralston, Osuna, and McManus.

Getting to Wimbledon

There was one difference between Ashe and the others, however: money. They had it and Ashe didn't. Some people were determined that Ashe should get there, however, including J. D. Morgan, who found some sponsors willing to help pay expenses. Dr. Johnson also raised some money, and the black high schools of Richmond took up a collection on Ashe's behalf.[3] Ashe also noted in *Off the Court* that a woman benefactor collected $800 for him to go to Wimbledon when he just mentioned that he was short of money for the trip. This happened at a white California country club, and Ashe was stunned by that act of generosity. "[F]or me it balanced the Balboa Club incident, which had shattered my image of California," he said.[4]

Ashe was all set for the Wimbledon trip, but before he could leave there was one piece of unfinished business in the intercollegiate circuit. That would be the National Intercollegiate Championships scheduled for Princeton, New Jersey, on June 22, 1963. Of course Ashe's airfare was paid to the East Coast, so he was able to save some on his ticket to England, since he and all of the other players were leaving directly after the championships. Out of a huge field of the best college tennis players in the nation, the quarterfinals came down to five players from USC or UCLA, one from Northwestern, and two from Texas universities.

When the quarterfinals were over, Texas representation was gone and facing off were Northwestern's Riessen against Osuna, and Ashe once again against Ralston. Ralston won the first two sets, 6–2 and 8–6, but to the surprise of many who thought Ralston would sweep, a determined Ashe came back to win the next two sets, 5–7 and 3–6. The next set was for the match and a berth in the finals. Ralston had been pushed to the edge by the upstart Ashe, but he had the big match experience, handled the pressure, and put Ashe away in the final, set 6–1. Once more, Ralston had defeated Ashe. And in the finals, Ralston disposed of Osuna, three sets to one.

It was disappointing, but for Ashe Wimbledon lay just ahead. Shortly after the Intercollegiates ended, many of its top players were on a plane winging to London. Arriving in the U.K. capital, Ashe was thrilled at being in his first foreign city. In the years to come, Ashe visited London many more times, and he grew extremely fond of the metropolis. He later wrote that "London is my favorite city and not simply because it was the first foreign city I visited. It appears to me the most civilized city in the world." The immense cultural amenities of the city, the politeness and fairness of its citizens, "despite their class consciousness," all impressed Ashe.[5]

If Ashe was impressed by London, he was in awe of Wimbledon. Arriving that first day at the All-England Lawn Tennis and Croquet Club, he was immediately struck by the sense of tradition, the ivy-green walls, the perfectly manicured grass courts, the nobility taking tea, and the uniforms of the linesmen with their straw hats—all virtually unchanged from a century ago.

Ashe's main college rival, USC's Dennis Ralston

The field was huge, with more than 170 players squaring off in the first round. All the pomp and mystique of Wimbledon had Ashe somewhat bewildered as he approached his first round match with Brazil's Carlos Fernandez on a remote outside court. He had trouble getting loose, and he lost the first two sets, 6–3 and 6–4. He was down in the third set but then fought his way back to take it, 6–4. Now with his confidence building, he stormed through the next two sets, 6–4 and 6–1, to take the match. It was his first Wimbledon victory, and he was exhilarated.[6]

Now he looked forward to his second-round match against Australia's John Hillebrand. That player was not well known, but he had a first-round win over another young comer named John Newcombe, who would one day be ranked the world's number-one player. The match may have drained Hillebrand, however, with one of the sets going twenty-six games and another going fifteen (this was before tiebreakers were introduced to finish a set). Nevertheless, Hillebrand was tough, the match going a long five sets, with Ashe prevailing for the win.

In his first Wimbledon, Ashe had reached the third round. He was quite pleased, but he knew his work was cut out for him when he saw his draw for the next match. It was Chuck McKinley, the number-one U.S. player. McKinley played for Trinity College in Texas, one of the country's hot tennis schools, but he had skipped the intercollegiate championships to come to England early and train for Wimbledon, where he would be a high seed.

McKinley's game was smoothed to a fine edge, and he beat the younger, less experienced Arthur in straight sets. Arthur was rather disconsolate at the loss, but he perked up when McKinley went to the finals and won without having lost one set in the entire tournament. At least Ashe had gone down to the very best. Putting McKinley's performance into perspective, one journal stated, "[T]o win the title in 21 straight sets is not a feat to be achieved by ordinary mortals."[7]

After Wimbledon

Ashe was satisfied with his first showing at Wimbledon, but he was awarded yet another international treat before heading back to the United States. Ashe and some of the his U.S. Wimbledon opponents, including Ralston and McKinley, were invited to play in a tournament in Sweden. The tennis players there were treated as top celebrities, and Ashe enjoyed several days of cordial Swedish hospitality, including dates with a couple of adoring fans. Ashe had to travel through Stockholm, the Swedish capital, and he would later count that city too among his favorite places. It was also Ashe's first experience with the midnight sun. He played one match at 9:30 P.M. in full daylight.[8]

Then it was back to the United States and the summer circuit with Forest Hills looming into view. There were some lesser tournaments before the big show at Forest Hills, however. Ashe did not fare particularly well in these, but he had some big individual wins over players seeded ahead of him, and even blew McKinley away, 6–1, in the first set of a match at Merion, Pennsylvania, eventually won by McKinley.

On the Davis Cup Team

During the early part of a tournament at South Orange, Ashe received the news he had been waiting all his life to hear. He was chosen for the Davis Cup team, the first African-American to be named to the American entry. It was a surprise, but not an overwhelming one. Although he had not won any big ones on the circuit, his overall record was quite respectable and the tennis elite saw that Ashe was coming on fast. They knew he was headed up in the rankings.

Still, some higher-ranked players, including Frank Froehling, Ham Richardson, Allen Fox, and Gene Scott had been left out. The other players chosen with Ashe were Chuck McKinley, Dennis Ralston, and Marty Riessen. Particularly distraught was Gene Scott, the number-eight U.S player, who said a USLTA executive had assured him that he would be chosen. To add insult to injury, Scott beat both Ashe and Riessen at South Orange.

There was some speculation at the time that Ashe was chosen because of his race—because it was the politically correct thing to do, but this suggestion was denied. The chairman of the selection committee stated, "Ashe was picked [for] his ability, not because of the color of his skin." Ashe was surrounded by reporters after the announcement, and he too refuted the idea that his selection represented a kind of tokenism.[9] Gene Scott was somewhat appeased when the committee announced that Scott would also join the team on its international trip, since Ashe had to return to UCLA. As newcomers on the team neither Scott, Ashe, nor Riessen were in line to play any significant matches.

Ashe's selection to the Davis Cup team was one of the great thrills of his life. In his memoir *Days of Grace*, he stated, "I . . . saw my Davis Cup appointment as the outstanding honor of my life to that point. Since no black had ever been on the team, I was now part of history."[10] Probably Ashe's only chance to play in 1963 would be against the Venezuela team in mid-September. Before that, however, there was the U.S. National Championships at Forest Hills. Ashe had not gone beyond the third round at Forest Hills, and once again he found himself in the third round, this time facing his Davis Cup teammate Marty Riessen. Ashe had beaten Riessen earlier in the summer, but at Forest Hills Riessen's game was sharp, and he took Arthur out in a tough match, 6–3, 8–6, 2–6, 8–6.

His first Davis Cup match came only a few days after Forest Hills. There had been a tough match against Mexico a few weeks earlier in which Ashe did not play, but the Americans cinched the tie (a series of Davis Cup matches is called a "tie") against Venezuela early, and Ashe was chosen for a relatively meaningless match against Orlando Braca-monte. Nevertheless, Ashe was tense. Although it was not an important match for the team, the consequences for Ashe were monumental. It would be the first time a black American represented the United States in the Davis Cup. Arthur had suffered the anguish of discrimination,

Ashe, shortly after being named to the Davis Cup team

but he still loved his country. Recalling that first match, Arthur would say, "Something reaches inside and squeezes your heart when you hear the umpire call 'Advantage United States,' instead of 'Advantage Ashe.' "[11]

Ashe's presence on the court the next day represented a breakthrough for African-Americans and a victory for all Americans in the struggle against racial intolerance. Bracamonte did not have a chance as an inspired Ashe, with cannon-shot serves, virtually destroyed him, 6–1, 6–1, 6–0. Over the next fifteen years, Ashe played in thirty-two Davis Cup matches and won twenty-seven of them, a record up to the time he retired.

The Davis Cup triumph had elevated Ashe's mood, and his performance at the Pacific Southwest Tournament at the end of September improved it further. The field included several top players and a promising newcomer, Stan Smith, who would become the top U.S. player as well as one of Ashe's best friends. Ashe blasted through the early opposition, not losing a set through the semis. Facing tough, highly ranked Rafael Osuna in the semifinal match, he looked unbeatable, blowing Osuna away 6–0 in the first set. But Osuna rallied and extended Ashe to 8–6 before succumbing. Ashe then went against Whitney Reed, the nation's number-six player, in the final. But Ashe continued his onslaught, overcoming a first set loss to win, 2–6, 9–7, 6–2.[12]

Ashe was returning to his junior year at UCLA on a high note. He knew his ranking would go up based on his recent performance and the Davis Cup membership, and he looked forward to studies and college tournament play. He was riding high, but there was trouble in the land. It was the 1960s, and the war in Vietnam was heating up; the country was starting to crack under the strain of antiwar protests; and Martin Luther King, Jr., was on the march, seeking rights for black Americans. Arthur had a lot of things to think about and some important decisions to make.

9

To the Top Rung of College Tennis

Arthur Ashe entered his junior year at UCLA as a big man on campus, a position he accepted gracefully. Still on the shy side, he had acquired national fame and even a smattering of international fame through the Davis Cup. When the November 1963 edition of *World Tennis* magazine came out, Ashe's fame increased. He was featured on the cover of that magazine, probably the most prestigious U.S. tennis publication of its time. The magazine apparently made its choice based purely on Ashe's record and placement on the Davis Cup squad. His ever-growing string of "firsts" as a black American tennis player seemingly did not enter into the decision.

As an upperclassman, Ashe could now live wherever he wanted, on or off campus, and with whom he pleased. After a bit of persuasion he chose to take an apartment near the campus with two tennis buddies, Charlie Pasarell and Jean Baker, who was from Haiti. The three spent time together out of the apartment as well, enjoying horseback riding, billiards, and Ping-Pong. Ashe's other friends included some of the hot UCLA basketball players such as Walt Hazzard, who later played for NBA Los Angeles Lakers, and Fred Frazier. They occasionally passed free time shooting baskets on the courts outside of Sproul Hall.

Up in the Ranks

Ashe had just turned twenty the previous July. Tennis was his world, and he was enjoying the increasingly luxurious lifestyle the sport provided. It got even better after the 1963 rankings came out at the end of the year. As much of the tennis world predicted, Ashe moved up in national ranking. He was now the number-six player in the United States, behind McKinley, Ralston, Froehling, Scott, and Riessen. And he was the first black American male to be ranked in the top ten. *World Tennis* magazine called him "probably 1963's most improved player." During the year, Ashe had twelve victories over top-twenty opponents, not to mention his Davis Cup appointment.[1]

Invitations to play in tournaments and exhibitions became more frequent, and Ashe accepted as many as his college schedule allowed. J. D. Morgan encouraged Ashe to take part in as many of these as he could, so that he could sharpen his game against top competition.

Exhibitions were especially welcome because there was no pressure to win and Ashe could enjoy the amenities of all-expenses-paid trips to some of the finest country clubs and resorts in the United States. Almost always they included a cocktail party, a fine dinner, and introductions to influential people. The USLTA also provided expense money for tournaments they sponsored. Not many invitations came from the South, but on the few occasions when Ashe was invited to a club in that region, he said that he suffered no outrageous treatment. Often, in both North and South, he was the only black person in the club, except for help. Ashe noticed that black waiters tended to give him the choicest cut of beef or the biggest steak, and he always got the best service.

Beyond Tennis

Junior year was decision time for Ashe. He knew what his major was going to be, but he had to decide about something else—something that would have far-reaching effects on his life and tennis career after college. The United States was in turmoil as the social and political issues of the 1960s heated up. There was concern over the increasing U.S. involvement in Vietnam, and many young men were being drafted to join the growing overseas contingent. In November 1963, the whole nation and much of the world came to a standstill at the news that President John F. Kennedy had been assassinated.

Ashe knew that he would be eligible for the draft right after college. Many students in those days were deferred from the draft as long as they stayed in college. Ashe had no problem with going into the Army, feeling it was the patriotic thing to do. At UCLA, every male student had to take two years of Reserve Officers Training Corps (ROTC). Now Ashe had to decide if he wanted to sign up for the next two years. That would be equivalent to enlisting in the Army because after graduation he would be obligated to a two-and-half-year hitch, with an automatic commission as second lieutenant.

His focus and discipline made Arthur Ashe military officer material.

After discussing the situation with his father, J. D. Morgan, and his Davis Cup captain, Ashe opted for the commission. They all agreed that Ashe would be better off going into the Army as an officer. Ashe was bright, fit, and disciplined—ideal officer material. The officer's training and development of leadership qualities would also serve him well in his career. For the young Arthur Ashe, who already had accomplished so much, it was another challenge, another opportunity to prove himself.[2]

Junior-Year Tennis

Ashe and Pasarell for the most part traded off the number-one position on the UCLA team during their junior year. Ashe was made co-captain of the team with David Reed. Between studies and the ROTC, Ashe played as much tournament tennis as possible. In December, at the National Hard Court Tournament, he did especially well against a field of outstanding national talent. As usual, USC and UCLA players, past and present, dominated play. Ashe met Allen Fox, a UCLA grad, in the final and took him out in two tough sets, 6–3 and 12–10, to claim the championship.

The U.S. National Indoor Championships at Salisbury, Maryland, came up in February and also drew an outstanding field, including such heralded foreign talent as Roy Emerson. Arthur made it to the quarterfinal round before being eliminated by Edlefsen of USC. A few weeks earlier, Ashe had made it to the finals of the Desert Invitation at Palm Beach only to be taken out once again by Ralston. The difference between Ashe's game and that of the players seeded above him was very slight at this point. He was right on the verge of being able to beat any player in the United States, and his game was still improving. *World Tennis* magazine, in its April 1964 issue, listed Ashe as the number-two player on the West Coast after Ralston.

As Ashe grew as a player, he also became more socially conscious. He began playing more charity exhibitions, sometimes even paying his own way to do so. Even then he was beginning to focus on helping children and was particularly disposed to playing in events for their benefit. Among the main beneficiaries of his activity, not surprisingly, was Dr. Johnson's Children's Development Fund. As his fame grew, Ashe did not forget the friends who had helped him along the way.

Ralston versus Ashe

In mid-March, at the Southern California Intercollegiates, Ashe lifted his game to a new level. By the quarterfinals, it was all USC versus UCLA. In the semis, Ashe beat USC's Bill Bond, while Ralston won over Pasarell. That set up a USC versus UCLA, Ralston versus Ashe, number-one versus number-two final. With school pride and bragging rights hanging in the balance, Ashe went after Ralston aggressively but lost the first set, 5–7. Unfazed, Ashe stayed with his game and won the second set, 6–4. It came down to a match set that went fourteen games. But this time Ashe held on and brought the victory home. Ashe, his teammates, and UCLA rejoiced.

Ralston, now a senior, did not have to wait long for a chance to avenge that loss. The Thunderbird Invitation at Phoenix, Arizona, came up on March 30, and the cream of Western tennis talent was there. This time Ashe met Ralston in the semis, but Ralston was prepared and won, 6–2, 6–4. Ralston might have relaxed after that, thinking he could take the final without too much effort against the lower-ranked Pasarell. That was a mistake. Arthur's roommate rose to the occasion, winning the final in three sets.[3]

With Ralston's college career winding down and Ashe about to go into his senior year, their abilities seemed to be evening out. Ashe defeated Ralston again in the finals of the AAWU tourney in April, and Ralston returned the compliment at the Southern California championships in May.

The National Intercollegiates in June marked the end of a brilliant college career for Dennis Ralston. The national tennis society rather expected another showdown between Ashe and Ralston, and they were not disappointed. The two friendly enemies squared off in the semis, both looking to take it all. For Ashe it was a last shot at winning the big one from Ralston. But it was Ralston's last hurrah, and he would not be denied, putting Arthur away, 6–3, 6–4, 6–3. In the finals, Ralston defeated Riessen to take the intercollegiate crown for the last time.

It might seem that Ashe was at war with his opponents on the court and that there would be great hostility between them. Quite the opposite was true, however. Off the court, Ashe was friendly with most of his opponents, even Dennis Ralston. Some of his toughest opponents, such as Stan Smith and Charlie Pasarell, became his best friends. In his writings, Arthur said that "so many of the people I know, especially the men I play against, are pretty damn good people."

Back at Wimbledon

With the college season over, Ashe looked forward to a second trip abroad. The magic of Wimbledon beckoned again. He had barely a chance to catch his breath before taking off for the All-England tourney, which began on July 4. Ashe was getting used to a pace that would become routine in the years that followed. He had no financial difficulties on this trip. Because of his high U.S. ranking and placement on the Davis Cup squad, the USLTA paid his expenses.

Ashe improved his performance over the previous year against a large, tough international field. The competition was so intense that many of the best American players, including Ralston, the fifth seed in the tournament, never made it to the second round. Ashe's serves and volleys were sharp on the fast Wimbledon grass, and he went into the second round against Cliff Richey, the young Texas phenom. Richey burst out of the blocks, and before Ashe knew what hit him he was suddenly down two sets and looking at elimination if he dropped the third. Ashe, as was his style, stayed cool, showing no reaction to the predicament. Richey was the one who got flustered when Ashe took the third set, 6–3. After that it was all Ashe, wrapping the match up, 6–2, 6–2.

Ashe made it through the third round, beating Billy Bond, but in the fourth round he faced the tourney's number-one seed and the world's acknowledged best player, Roy Emerson. Ashe kept his composure, but Emerson eliminated him in straight sets, although Ashe threatened in the third set before going down, 7–5.[4] Arthur did gain some confidence from that last set and felt that the time might not be far off when he would beat the number-one Australian. Emerson went on to win the tourney.

Later in the tournament, Ashe matched up with Billy Bond in doubles and had his first opportunity to play on Wimbledon's center court. It was also the first time—but not the last—that Arthur would go through the ritual of walking out on the court, turning to the royal box, and bowing to the members of the royal family who were present. Ashe and Bond did not do so well in the match, losing in five sets, but the third set turned out to be longest Arthur had ever played, going forty-two games before Ashe-Bond eked out a set win.

This time around, Ashe did not have to skimp so much and he was better able to enjoy London, including the night life. He and his friends went out on the town and even took in some of the London nightlife. At the grand ball honoring Wimbledon's finest, Ashe watched the men's and women's winners dance the first dance and envisioned that one day he might have that traditional honor. After the ball, there was a tournament in Hungary during which Ashe celebrated his twenty-first birthday.

Finishing College

The highlight of the summer circuit was the Eastern Grass Court Tournament, which Ashe won, beating Clark Graebner in the finals. It was another honor for Ashe, who became the first black American male to win a major grass-court tournament. Then it was on to Forest Hills, where he again got knocked out in the third round, this time by Marty Riessen. Emerson was again the eventual winner.

Back at UCLA, Ashe dug in for his senior year. At the end of 1964, the new national rankings came out and Ashe was now rated the number-three player in the United States. He was further honored by being named captain of the UCLA team. All these honors notwithstanding, he trained harder than ever in anticipation of the college season. This year, however, one of the major roadblocks for Ashe and UCLA had been removed. Dennis Ralston had graduated and moved on. Ashe continued to meet Ralston in non-collegiate tournaments, but without his big nemesis to contend with, Arthur swept through the college circuit in the spring of 1965. He won both the intercollegiate singles and (with Ian Crookenden) doubles championships, and thus allowed UCLA to wrest the college title away from USC. He finished the season with a 35–4 record in singles. Arthur Ashe was now clearly the number-one player in the college ranks.[5]

His college playing days were over. The tall, skinny kid from Richmond had come a long way, but his biggest battles still lay ahead.

10

The Australian Conquest

Arthur Ashe's collegiate playing days may have been over at the end of his fourth college year, but he still had to graduate. The demands of the intercollegiate tennis schedule and the temptation to play high-profile tournaments had taken its toll on his academic work, and Ashe still needed nine credit hours for his degree. He wanted to finish his degree work, but other tempting opportunities were coming up, and he found himself at a crossroads once again. Finally, he decided to postpone his return to the classroom until the spring of 1966. It was a Davis Cup offer that turned his head. The team was planning to tour Australia, and Ashe, in his third year on the U.S. squad, was invited along. The tour would be not only a great travel adventure, but also an opportunity to face the high-ranking Australians in major tournaments.

The Australian trip was scheduled for the fall. Before that, however, Ashe had to deal with his third Wimbledon trip and the summer circuit. At Wimbledon he made it into the fourth round, his best showing yet at the All-England event. For the round of sixteen, he found himself matched against Rafael Osuna, the Mexican champ who had been Ralston's teammate at USC. Maybe Ashe remembered the days when Osuna and Ralston were nearly unbeatable at USC. In any case, he lost to Osuna in straight sets. After that,

Ashe just couldn't seem to get his game going. On the summer circuit, he met Ralston several times and lost each time.

United States versus Mexico

Then came a turning point. The Davis Cup tie against Mexico was on the horizon, and Ashe was scheduled to play. It would be only his third Davis Cup match, although it was his third year on the team. Almost two years had elapsed before he played his second match, one with Canada, in which he had two wins. Canada was not too tough, but Mexico was a major roadblock on the way to the Cup finals. The United States had won the Cup in 1963 but lost it to Australia the next year, and they were eager for a rematch. Before that, except for two years, the Aussies had dominated Cup play since 1950. The Mexico tie was scheduled for Dallas, where summer heat is always a factor.

The Davis Cup captain George McCall picked Ashe to face the first Mexican opponent on opening day. The first match is always important, giving a team the opening edge, so McCall was showing great confidence in Ashe. Arthur was not so confident when he saw who his draw was against: none other than Osuna, who had just beaten him easily at Wimbledon and had usually beaten him in college matches. The Mexican team figured they had a big edge. But Ashe was playing for his team and his country now, not just for himself. Pancho Gonzalez had also come on board as a coach, and he had Ashe's serve humming. In the blistering heat, Ashe dug deep for something extra and overpowered a weakening Osuna in straight sets. It was a stunning upset, leaving the Mexicans in shock. They never seemed to recover their composure as the Americans overwhelmed them to take the tie, capping it off with another win by Ashe.

At Forest Hills

Ashe's accomplishments were not overlooked by the USLTA. In the U.S. Championships at Forest Hills that year, he was seeded fifth. That meant he would be at center court and in the spotlight throughout the tournament. There was more gala and hype than usual because it was the tourney's fiftieth anniversary. More than 300 players registered for the event. Ashe, gaining more confidence now, went as far as he had ever gone at Forest Hills, reaching the quarterfinals. Then things really got tough.

His draw for the quarterfinal match was Roy Emerson, who he had never beaten and who had eliminated Ashe at both Forest Hills and Wimbledon. Emerson had been the number-one ranking player in the world since 1962 and was top seed in the tournament. Despite all that, Arthur went into the match with confidence. He had received some sound coaching and felt like a breakthrough was possible. "I felt more confident than I ever had before," he later wrote. "It was hard to explain, because I also knew that I'd never before in my life played well enough to beat Emerson."[1]

Right from the beginning, Ashe went on the offensive. His serve was hot, and he powered back Emerson's returns, leaving the Australian a bit ruffled. He was also careful not to make foolish mistakes, or unforced errors, as they are called in tennis. When Ashe won the first two sets, the gallery started to buzz. Could young Ashe, barely out of the college circuit, actually upset the acknowledged best tennis player in the world? But "Emmo," as he was called, was a battler, and the crowd expected him to fight his way back into the match. Fight he did, and after twenty-two games Emerson finally pulled the third set out, 12–10. But Ashe smelled victory and would not let go. Changing his strategy, he slowed his game down, confusing Emerson who, now trying too hard, double-faulted repeatedly. In the end, Ashe was the victor, 6–2, pulling off his second major upset of the summer.

Ashe had been "the" black tennis player in the world, the one to watch, but now suddenly he was the hottest topic in tennis, and it had nothing to do with his skin color. News of his victory rang around the world. Reporters clamored

Enjoying his victory over Roy Emerson to win the South Australian
tennis championship in 1965

for interviews, and Ralph Bunche, a U.S. diplomat and a major leader of black Americans, personally congratulated him. The win made the front page of *Richmond News Leader,* a hometown black-American newspaper, and Arthur Ashe, Sr., picked up and headed for New York to see his son play in the semifinals.

Ashe became the great hope to regain the U.S. title, which had not been held by an American since 1955. For his opponent he drew Manuel Santana, the leading player from Spain. Arthur took the court still flushed with his triumph over Emerson. Santana, however, was a skillful player and had no intention of matching Ashe's power game. He played with finesse and attacked Ashe's weakness, his low-ball volleys.[2] Two years earlier, *World Tennis* magazine had stated that "Ashe . . . will do well as soon as he learns to get down for the ball."[3] And six months after the Santana match, a *New York Times* article said, "The nearest thing he has to a weakness is his low volley. . . ."[4] Exploiting that weakness, Santana took a disappointed Ashe out in straight sets.

Worldwide Tennis

After Forest Hills, Ashe continued on the circuit, playing with a fury and winning some eight of his next fourteen tournaments. The next Davis Cup tie was scheduled for October 1965 against Spain in Barcelona. Spain played on clay so the American team was at an immediate disadvantage, particularly Ashe. McCall invited Ashe along with the team, but all Ashe got out of it was a good trip, because McCall recognized that Ashe's power game was not good on clay. It didn't matter much; the Spanish team made short work of the Americans anyway, knocking them out of contention for the Cup. The team was downhearted at being eliminated, but they looked forward with relish to the Australia trip, which began with a stop off in New Zealand.

Before the journey began, however, McCall gave the team a new financial deal that helped relieve Ashe's rather chronic money shortage. Under the new plan, each player would receive year-round a stipend of $20 per day and $28 for tournament days. And, of course, all travel and lodging expenses were paid. For Ashe, it provided a steady source of income. For McCall, it meant having control over the players twelve months a year rather than just during tournaments. He now had the power to schedule where and when the players played, whether in Davis Cup ties or other tourneys. It curtailed the individual freedom of the players but promoted team unity.

"My first Australian tour was a blast," Ashe stated in his writings.[5] The tour would be a long one, three months, with all of the matches on grass. In New Zealand, the intellectually curious Ashe enjoyed observing the Maoris—the aboriginal peoples of New Zealand—and studying the island's unusual flora and fauna. From the time he was absorbed in his *National Geographic* magazines as a young boy, Ashe was intensely interested in foreign cultures, and wherever he traveled throughout his life he always tried to experience the local customs. After a few days in which they played several exhibitions, it was off to Australia and a showdown with the Aussie rackets.

In his observations about the Australians, Ashe noted the British influences but stated that "there was none of the English snottiness. The Australians were fiercely middle class and quick to put down any attempts at snobbishness or pretension." Of course, being an African-American who had been exposed to racism, Ashe was quickly aware of Australian attitudes toward the Aborigines. The discriminatory treatment of the Aborigines, the original peoples of Australia, was more comparable to the sufferings of American Indians than to African-Americans, however. Ashe was treated quite well in Australia, especially by the Australian press.

Looking back on that first Australian trip, Ashe considered it "as important to my tennis career as meeting Dr. Johnson and living in St. Louis during my senior year in high school."[6] Arthur quite amazingly took Australia by storm. A headline in the December 1965 issue of *World Tennis* blared:

Arthur Ashe Beats the Entire
Australian Davis Cup Team

Indeed, after an opening-day loss to Emerson, Ashe trounced Fred Stolle, John Newcombe, and then Emerson in the final. Ashe's service was so potent that he was dubbed "Aces Ashe." Stolle, the world's number-two rated amateur, was especially victimized as Ashe peppered him with twenty-one aces (an ace being a serve that an opponent cannot return). *World Tennis* reported that "within a matter of five days Arthur Ashe so completely thrashed the Champion Nation's top three players in winning the Queensland Singles Championship that any complacency that previously existed . . . was shattered."[7]

Over the next three months, Ashe continued on a rampage, winning the South Australian Championship in Adelaide, the Western Australian in Perth, and the Tasmanian Championship in Hobart. During this time, leading up to the Australian National Championships, Ashe lived mostly in Sydney, enjoying that city's ambiance. He socialized with Australian tennis players, went to movies, clubs, and restaurants, and he enjoyed the classical and popular music so plentiful in Sydney. He also dated Australian girls and even blamed one relationship for one of his few bad outings. In an interview with *The New York Times Magazine,* he said that his mind wandered during a match with John Newcombe. This was the same problem that cropped up occasionally at UCLA, but J. D. Morgan was not here to bawl him out. Apparently Ashe had met Bella, a flight attendant from Trinidad, and he could not stop thinking about her during the match. Although he started out beating Newcombe, his lack of concentration eventually spelled his doom.

Apart from that one lapse, Ashe played splendidly in Australia and went into the final championship round with

91

momentum. The great press he was getting made him a high-profile celebrity, and he was in constant demand for television and other media interviews. He reached the finals of the Australian National Championship, where he once again faced the daunting Emerson. Ashe was eager for the match, but a rainstorm caused a one-day cancellation, and the twenty-four-hour delay gave the normally calm Ashe a case of the jitters. When he stepped on the court, his confidence lagged, and Emmo was in top form. In the end, Emerson emerged victorious, and Ashe, by now a bit homesick, looked forward to the long flight back to the United States. He would finish off his degree in June and then go directly into the Army. What Army life would hold for him he could only guess.

11

∞

From Tennis White to Army Khaki

With the Australian tour under his belt, Ashe returned to the United States the conquering hero. Not only had he beaten Australia's best, but when the 1965 U.S. rankings came out, he was in the number-two position, after Dennis Ralston. Ralston's dominance over Ashe seemed to be continuing beyond their college rivalry. Still, Ashe was elated and felt in his heart that his day would come. Right now he had to concentrate on getting back to UCLA and finishing off those nine credit hours for his degree.

Arthur Ashe Day

Then something happened that stunned Arthur Ashe. He got a call from Richmond. The city, now ready to reclaim its native son, had declared an "Arthur Ashe Day" on February 22, 1966. Ashe felt honored, of course, but he had mixed feelings as well. After all, Richmond was the city that would not let him play in its all-white tennis facilities or enter its all-white tournaments. Now that he was a national celebrity, the city fathers were welcoming him back. He could have turned it down, but his old friend and first tennis coach, Ron Charity, was promoting the event. And, more important, the proceeds of the day were earmarked for the Junior Development Fund of the American Tennis Association. Ashe had benefited from that fund, and he was more than willing to give something back. There would be

93

a banquet in his honor and a tournament including some of the nation's top tennis stars.

Ashe enjoyed returning to Richmond a hero. He was the focus of attention, and praise was heaped upon him from all quarters. He was greeted by the mayor on the City Hall steps, received a resolution from the City Council declaring Arthur Ashe Day, and appeared before the legislature to accept more honors. To resounding applause at the banquet he said, "This is the biggest day of my life."[1]

The next day the tournament took place and, ironically, Ashe did not do well. All the hype, the old friends, and the memories distracted him, and if ever he could not focus on a game it was on that day. He was amazed too by the changes in Richmond. He wrote: "The one-time capital of the Confederacy was honoring a descendant of slaves. Racially mixed tennis matches were now possible in the city that barred me from going to school with white children, or from playing on tennis courts used by whites." And now here he was playing in Richmond's first major tournament that allowed mixed races. But through all the pomp and ceremony, there was no word of apology from the city for its past treatment of blacks. He lost to Frank Froehling that day, and after it was all over he went with his father and stepmother back to the house on Sledd Street in Brook Field where it had all begun.[2]

Preparing for Military Life

Ashe devoted the next three months to hitting the books rather than tennis balls. He kept his tennis sharp by working out with the team, coaching the freshmen, and helping J. D. Morgan recruit. Although Ashe devoted himself to academics throughout the spring, the Davis Cup coach insisted that he play some tournaments to keep his game up. That made studying tougher, but Arthur managed to pass his courses, and he graduated in June. Now there was time to sneak in one more Wimbledon before his Army commitment began, and he took off for England within hours of finishing his exams. It was a rather token gesture, however, since he had so little tournament play in the previous three months. That year, 1966, Santana won over Ralston in the finals.

When Ashe returned, he immediately reported to the ROTC training camp at Fort Lewis, Washington. That July he turned twenty-three. The program at Fort Lewis was equivalent to U.S. Army basic training, presumably designed to make soldiers out of civilians. Arthur was in good physical shape, but the demands of basic training are beyond what almost any civilian ever has to endure. In addition, basic training attempts to strip recruits of any ego or feelings of self-importance they may bring into camp, so they can be reprogrammed the Army way. They are harassed, humiliated, and dehumanized; made to do the meanest, lowliest tasks; and forced to listen to the harshest criticism without talking back.

This was really tough on Ashe, who was just getting used to the celebrity treatment accorded the nation's second-ranking tennis player and the world's sixth. However, the strong disciplinary training Ashe got from his father and Dr. Johnson may have helped. Ashe got through the six tough weeks anyway, as most recruits do, and was awarded his commission as a second lieutenant in the army. Now the question was: How was Lieutenant Ashe to be assigned?

The Army brass had already been considering the best way to use Lieutenant Arthur Ashe. The Army generally tries to utilize any special skills its soldiers may possess. In Ashe's case, the decision was quick. He was assigned to West Point, the U.S. Military Academy, as the data processing officer, for which he would take further training; he would also serve as assistant tennis coach. The setup gave Ashe time to practice in the evenings, and he was allowed to participate in some tournaments, including Davis Cup play. This would be good for Ashe—his tennis career would not have to suffer while he was in the Army—and it would be good public relations for the Army. After all, Ashe would be representing the United States in the Davis Cup, and it would be almost unpatriotic not to let him play.

Surveying the tennis courts at West Point

In the meantime, Ashe had taken a rather large step in another direction. When he was at UCLA in the spring, it was not only his studies that he was serious about, but also Pat Battles, his longtime girl friend from the East Coast. In March 1966, they announced their engagement, and when Ashe moved to West Point, the two were able to see more of each other. Ashe, however, began to have second thoughts. He was a lieutenant in the Army now, he had traveled all over the world, and he looked forward to even more worldwide adventures. The idea of being tied down in his early twenties did not sit well with him. In March 1967, he broke the engagement.[3]

Davis Cup Play

Ashe's military years were tough ones for the U.S. Davis Cup team. In a 1966 tie with Jamaica, Ashe won both his matches, but he and Cliff Richey lost in the doubles to Lance Lumsden and Richard Russell, one of the only other ranked black players in the hemisphere. It was Ashe's first Davis Cup loss, and the triumph was monumental for Jamaica. The whole of the West Indies exploded in celebration.

In November, the team was upset by Brazil on that country's home court. Ashe won in doubles with Ralston, but McCall made a controversial decision to start Cliff Richey in singles instead of Ashe, and Richey got trounced. Into his decision, McCall factored the Brazilians' clay courts, their heavier ball, and Richey's better record on clay. Nevertheless, Ashe was higher ranked overall than Richey, and many people questioned the decision not to use him. In reflection, McCall's decision seemed even more questionable when Ashe subsequently won the U.S. Clay Court Championship.

The next year brought an even greater shock, made more so because the American team was doing well, having beaten the Mexican team again, and this time on their own clay turf. Ashe, having repeated for 1966 as the number-two U.S. amateur behind teammate Ralston, again defeated the frustrated Osuna in straight sets. Now they were scheduled to play a weaker Ecuadorian team in the zone finals in Guayaquil, again on clay. To everyone's surprise the Eucadorians rose up and swatted the highly favored U.S. team, eliminating them from Cup competition.[4] Remarking on that series, Ashe said, "My losses to Miguel Olvera and Pancho Guzman in that series have to rank as one of the low points of my career. . . ."[5]

Lieutenant Ashe may have also been a little disappointed at not being able to move up in the USLTA rankings. At the end of 1967, he was again in the number-two spot, but this time it was his old pal Charlie Pasarell who was at the top of the amateur heap. Pasarell received the honor on the basis of his winning the U.S. National Indoor

Championship in singles and doubles. Ironically, his partner in doubles was none other than Lieutenant Arthur Ashe. Pasarell also had won the indoor singles in 1966, beating Ashe in the finals. Ashe may still have felt he was cheated because for two years in a row he had been number two to Ralston, and now Ralston had turned pro, leaving Ashe the heir-apparent. Ashe also may have felt he deserved to be ranked higher because he was the U.S. Clay Court champ. The poor showing of the Davis Cup team, however, may have been the deciding factor.[6]

Thinking of Turning Pro

Arthur was supporting himself very well during his Army service. He had his lieutenant's pay, and of course his housing and clothing costs were taken care of by the Army as well. The Davis Cup team also provided a stipend for its members, so money was no longer really a problem in Ashe's life. In addition, even before he went into the Army, his name had grown big enough that corporations now looked to him for endorsements. He drank Coca-Cola in public for that company, used a Wilson tennis racket, gave tennis clinics for Wilson Sporting Goods, and wore tennis outfits made by Fred Perry Tennis Togs. His contracts with these companies paid him an annual retainer. Philip Morris Incorporated hoped to sign Ashe to a contract as soon as he left the service in 1968. None of these deals affected Arthur's amateur standing, as most of the top amateurs had similar deals. This was a point of contention among many observers, however, who felt it made a sham of amateurism.

Turning pro was something Ashe had already thought about. The top amateurs were turning pro with increasing regularity, and the money to be made was becoming more and more attractive. Before 1968, pros had their own circuit and did not play against amateurs. Amateurs like Ashe hesitated to turn pro because the pros were locked out of amateur tournaments such as Wimbledon and the U.S. and French Championships, which still had the highest prestige in the sport. There was considerable clamoring from many quarters that the line between pros and amateurs be abolished and that they should all be allowed to play in the same tournaments.

International Lawn Tennis Association (ILTA) officials had long been resistant to open tennis competition that would mix pros and amateurs, but they were beginning to wilt. They could see that they were excluding some of the world's best players—Ralston, Emerson, and Laver among them—and that this situation would only grow worse. In October 1967, Britain had announced unilaterally that it would make Wimbledon an open tournament, so it seemed other competitions would have to follow. The following March, the ILTA voted unanimously for open tennis. A month later, the first open tournament was held at Bournemouth, England, and the USLTA scheduled its first open for Forest Hills.[7]

Ashe looked forward to open tennis and ending the confusion between amateurs and pros. After beating Emerson in straight sets at Madison Square Garden in March 1968, Ashe told *The New York Times*, "When I do get out of the Army, I'm going to have to turn pro if open tennis is here." Indeed, it did come, and it set up an unusual situation in U.S. tennis in 1968. For that year there would be both amateur and open championships, and Lieutenant Ashe was scheduled to play in both.

12

Historic 1968

The year 1968 proved to be a monumental one for the United States and for Arthur Ashe as well. It was a year when the war raged on in Vietnam and student antiwar protests swept the America. It was the year that North Vietnam's Tet offensive told the American people that the war would not end soon and President Lyndon Johnson withdrew from the presidential race. It was the year that the Democratic Convention in Chicago was thrown into chaos by protests and riots in the streets outside. And it was the year U.S. astronauts first orbited the moon. Tragically, it was also the year in which Martin Luther King, Jr., and Robert Kennedy were assassinated.

Speaking Out

It was difficult not to become politicized in 1968, and especially hard for a young, aware black American. In March of that year, Arthur Ashe took his first big step into the political world. He was asked to make a speech on black responsibility at a Washington, D.C., church. In the past, Ashe had avoided involvement in political and civil rights matters, although he felt strongly about both. Ashe at first refused the speaking engagement, saying truthfully that it was against Army policy for him to make a political speech. But when the church leaders challenged him, he gave in and made the speech. It was a year when people were speaking out in large numbers, especially about the war and civil rights, and Ashe also believed he needed to express what he thought and felt in those tumultuous times.

When the Army brass heard of the speech, Ashe was reprimanded, but he was glad that he had spoken out. He later wrote, "The speech released a great deal of anxiety and guilt I had repressed and marked the beginning of a period of political activity—in and out of tennis." Ashe had lived the good life that tennis offered even while in the Army, but the events of 1968 brought things to a head. Knowing that young soldiers were injured or dying while he remained stationed at West Point was also stressful. And knowing that many young blacks were paying with their lives for the questionable U.S. foreign policy turned Ashe against the Southeast Asian conflict even while he was in the Army.[1]

The civil rights movement was coming to tennis too. In August 1968, it came to light in the media that certain Washington, D.C., country clubs, which counted high-ranking government officials among their membership, would not admit black members or play other country club teams that included blacks. The controversy centered around an African-American woman, Mrs. Carl T. Rowan, whose husband, then a syndicated columnist, was a former ambassador to Finland and former head of the United States Information Agency. Mrs. Rowan played on her club's B tennis team, but rather than play that team, several all-white clubs dropped B tennis.

Mr. Rowan, in response, commented that "We found it morbidly funny that at the time this nation was deeply involved in a great struggle in Southeast Asia, when the great cities were facing chaos and decay . . . that the supposedly elite people of this country could be running around holding secret meetings to figure out how to keep one Negro woman off a tennis court." Hugely embarrassed by the exposure, the clubs were forced to change their policies.[2]

On the Court

Arthur performed outstandingly well in 1968 in both Davis Cup and individual competition, courtesy of the U.S. Army. At Wimbledon 1968 he had his best showing to date, soaring into the semifinals on the crest of wins over John Newcombe and Tom Okker, the Netherlands ace. In the semis he faced Rod Laver, now a pro in this first open Wimbledon. Laver, whom Ashe considered the best tennis player ever, whipped Ashe in straight sets. Over the years, Laver dominated Ashe as no other player had, beating him seventeen successive times. The Australian went on to take the Wimbledon crown that year. Ashe did not despair, knowing he was in good form for the matches coming up, particularly Davis Cup play, the U.S. National Amateur Championship, and the first U.S. Open at Forest Hills.

By a freak of scheduling, the Davis Cup tie against Spain in Cleveland was set to finish just in time for the start of the amateur championships in mid-August. The Open would follow only a week later. The schedule could not be more grueling. It was hot and muggy in Cleveland for the Davis Cup competition, but the newly assembled Davis Cup team, led by new captain Donald Dell, looked like the best American group in years. They defeated the Spanish team, with Ashe winning over Santana in a final heroic battle that went eighty-three games and had to be completed the next day. It broke the record for the longest Cup match played to date.[3]

The next day Ashe, near exhaustion, found himself on the court again in the National Amateur Championships in Brookline, Massachusetts. He barely got by an unknown in the first round and then managed a day of rest. Ashe beat old friend Jim McManus in the semis and went up against another comrade, Bob Lutz, in the final. Lutz played superbly, but it was Ashe's day despite a searing 100°F (38°C) court temperature. In fact, the temperature probably favored Ashe because his Army fitness training had put him in the best condition of his life. Arthur slammed twenty aces past Lutz to capture the crown he had tried nine times

102

Ashe shaking hands with Tom Okker after defeating him in the
quarterfinals at Wimbledon, 1968

to achieve. He was heralded the best amateur in the land, virtually assured of the number-one ranking. Lieutenant Ashe was also the first American to hold the amateur title since Tony Trabert in 1955.[4] Ashe would have to prove himself again, however, in the tourney that lay just ahead.

The ironic sidelight to his victory was that it came on the same day as the disclosure that those exclusive Washington country clubs had dropped out of a tennis league rather than play against a black woman. It prompted Arthur to say that he would not be allowed membership in "seven-eighths" of the American clubs where he was booked for tournaments. *The New York Times* commented, "It is eleven years since Althea Gibson won at Wimbledon and Forest Hills, but it is shockingly obvious that those who run many American country clubs do not yet know the score."[5]

At the U.S. Open

It was the first U.S. Open, and the excitement level was high. The huge field was a virtual "Who's Who" of the tennis world. Even graying Pancho Gonzalez showed up and still had enough left to power his way into the quarterfinals. Ashe was now playing the best tennis of his life, but the task ahead was formidable. Seeded ahead of him were four world-class Australian pros: Laver, Tony Roche, Ken Rosewall, and John Newcombe. And right behind him were his fellow Davis Cuppers: Emerson, Ralston (now a pro), Cliff Drysdale from South Africa, the Dutch Tom Okker, Gonzalez, Clark Graebner, and a host of others.

Ashe worried most of all about how he would get by Laver, but that turned out not to be a problem. Drysdale, in a stunning upset, took Laver out of the tournament in the fourth round. Everyone, including Ashe, was in disbelief over that outcome. It took the number-one seed out, but the road ahead was still tough. In that same round, Arthur had to face Emerson, but his power game was on course, and he managed to get by the former champion, 6–4, 9–7, 6–3.[6]

Ashe had made it into the quarterfinals, and the draw matched him against the Laver-vanquisher, Drysdale. This

Ashe with a backhand return to Cliff Drysdale
at Forest Hills, 1968

was more than just two men meeting on a tennis court. Arthur, a free black American, would square off against a South African, whose country still embraced apartheid, an official policy of segregation and subjugation of non-white peoples. Although there was some pressure on Ashe to boycott the match, he went ahead and played, refusing to be directed or used by outside forces. He would one day confront apartheid directly, but he would always judge the South African players on individual merit. Cliff Drysdale was one he grew close to in later years. On the courts that day, however, Ashe was all business, and he sent Drysdale packing, 8–10, 6–3, 9–7,6–4.[7]

He had reached the semifinals in this cataclysmic year of 1968. Now he would face his Davis Cup teammate Clark Graebner. This was a clash between power players,

Graebner's serve being almost a match for Arthur's. The two were also look-alikes in one respect; they both sported the same dark-framed horn-rimmed glasses while they played. The match began with Graebner's serve dominating play, as he drilled ace after ace and took the first set. He was ahead in the second set when Ashe at set point uncharacteristically sent a lob over Graebner's head, leaving him helpless at the net. Arthur took that set and then, leaving his usual game, mixed lobs, dinks, and chips with his power strokes to take the next two sets and propel himself into the finals.

The finals matched Ashe against Tom Okker, who had beaten the last pro standing in the tournament, Ken Rosewall. As Ashe waited at center court for the signal to begin, he realized that he stood at the brink of his greatest achievement in tennis. In the stands were his father and Dr. Johnson, who had come up for the occasion. Donald Dell and Dick Savitt, a former Wimbledon champion, coached him before and through the match, Dell telling him to get his first serve in and make the first volley, and Savitt imploring him to stay low and bend his knees.

To comply, Ashe crouched and did deep knee bends before Okker's serve. Dell need not have worried about Arthur's serve; it was sizzling and on target. He served fifteen aces in a hard-fought first set before winning, 14–12. Okker took the second and fourth sets and Arthur the third. It came down to the fifth set and Ashe, serving to Okker's backhand, went up, 5–2. Ashe took the last game on his serve without losing a point, serving up his twenty-sixth ace on his way to winning the match.

So Ashe stood alone at the top of world-class tennis players. Briefly, he held his clasped hands aloft like a boxer who has just won a fight, then he quickly regained his composure. Later he wrote, "The award ceremony that day will always hold a special place in my heart. My father came onto the court with me and it felt wonderful to share that moment with him. . . . Bob Kelleher introduced me as 'General Ashe' as I laughed and hugged my father. He was crying."[8]

At the net and on his way to a 1968 U.S. Open victory over Tom Okker

Dave Anderson of *The New York Times* said it was "the most notable achievement made in the sport by a Negro male athlete."[9] When Ashe returned to West Point, the cadets in the Great Hall gave him a three-and-a-half-minute ovation, a rare honor at the Point. So amazing was his feat that the next week he became the first athlete (let alone the first black athlete) to appear on TV's "Face the Nation." People wanted to hear from Arthur Ashe now, not just about tennis, but about his views on black athletes and civil rights, as well. Ten days after his victory, he appeared on the cover of *Life* magazine. The handsome bachelor became a contestant on TV's "The Dating Game" and also appeared as a guest on "The Joey Bishop Show." Arthur Ashe had come a long way from Richmond.[10]

Even though there was $100,000 in prize money to be distributed among the Open winners, Arthur, still an amateur and an Army officer, collected only his $28-a-day stipend, and the USLTA paid for his hotel room. Okker was technically an amateur, but he was allowed to "register" as a pro and thus was eligible for the first-place prize money of $14,000. The "registered player" category was dropped soon thereafter.

The 1968 Davis Cup

That fall, the Davis Cup team beat India and qualified for the challenge round against Australia. The U.S. team had experienced a five-year drought in the Cup, and now they were just one tie away from bringing it home. The unbeaten Americans were favored this time, the best Australian players having turned pro. After Graebner and Ashe won the first two matches, only one more win was needed to secure the Cup. Ashe was on the verge of seeing another of his dreams fulfilled, having his name etched on the Davis Cup. The last match was a doubles contest, with Stan Smith and Bob Lutz representing the Americans, and the winner would take home the Cup.

Arthur and Graebner drove around Adelaide listening to the match on the radio, too nervous to sit in one place in the stadium. When the winning point was announced, it was a hugely emotional moment for Ashe. He would later describe his reaction: "The dream had come true. All the hours and days of travel, practice, strange hotel rooms, foreign accents, aching shins and elbows had converged on this point in time. It was worth it. We had won the Davis Cup."[11]

Enjoying Success

Now Ashe had attained a whole new level of life. On the way back from Australia under State Department protection, the team toured Southeast Asia and were hosted by General Creighton Abrams. They visited hospitals and played exhibitions. Once, they were so close to the action

The 1969 Davis Cup victors (left to right): Ashe, Donald Dell, and Clark Graebner

while playing that they could see and hear mortar shell explosions. The trip made Ashe even more adamantly opposed to the war, despite General Abrams's explanations.

Ashe had to interrupt the trip to return home for a special event. He had been voted one of America's Ten Outstanding Young Men by the Jaycees. Of course, the same group had not let him play in their tournaments eight years earlier. Afterward, Ashe eagerly rejoined his comrades in Southeast Asia. When they finally returned home, the team met with President and Lady Bird Johnson, and they also met Democratic candidate Hubert Humphrey, whom Ashe came to admire. Humphrey so impressed Ashe that the tennis player began thinking that he too might one day enter politics. On a tour of France with the team, Ashe spent Thanksgiving with Sargent Shriver and met his mother-in-law, Rose Kennedy, mother of John and Robert Kennedy, both killed by assassins' bullets.[12]

Arthur Ashe was riding high in a whole new world. That world changed again in February 1969, when he was discharged from the Army and announced that he would turn pro. Shortly before that, Ashe had received another honor he had always sought: he was ranked number one in the United States.

13

§

Finding
a Way

It was the last year of the 1960s, and Arthur Ashe had stepped into his new life as a pro. It was not that much different from his amateur career, now that open tennis had been accepted. Unlike pros before the open period, Ashe would be going on the same tours, playing many of the same tournaments as he did as an amateur, and he would be playing the pro circuit as well. Ashe's pro career took off quickly, propelled by his 1968 victories and the avalanche of publicity that came with them. His fame was all the greater because he was the first and only black American in the top echelon of tennis. An *Ebony* magazine article stated that "Thus in a non-team sport with no other black star, Arthur Ashe is the whole black race."[1]

A More Complicated Life

Ashe's travel schedule became even more crowded between playing pro tournaments and continuing with the Davis Cup team, which now accepted pros. Added to those were State Department goodwill junkets all over the world, as the U.S. government looked to Ashe to represent the country. Ashe's life was really getting quite complicated now, considering the number of corporations that began vying for his services. He needed someone to help manage his affairs, and that person was Donald Dell, the Davis Cup captain, who had acquired a law degree. Dell, seeing the wealth of tennis stars rapidly growing, established a business in which he advised and represented top tennis pros such as Ashe, Stan Smith, and others in their business negotiations. He knew his clients personally from his own tennis background, and he became one of Ashe's best and most trusted friends. For much of their twenty-year association, Ashe and Dell never had a contract, all arrangements being sealed by a handshake.[2] Donald Dell was certainly a major groundbreaker in the multimillion-dollar sports agenting business that exists today.

In the years immediately after his U.S. Open victory, Ashe made a number of notable corporate connections. One of these was with the tennis racket company Head, for whom Ashe helped develop a signature racket. Another was with the Catalina company, with whom Ashe helped break "the color line" in tennis clothing. Ashe insisted on wearing that company's colorful tennis wear rather than the traditional white ruled by the USLTA, and eventually the regulation was changed. He also became the pro at the Doral Country Club, went into a management-training program at Philip Morris, and did tennis clinics for American Airlines and for a tennis sports camp headed by Nick Bollettieri. Working at the Doral also gave Ashe the opportunity to play golf, a game that he came to love.[3] In *Portrait in Motion*, he stated that he would not play tennis on his wedding day, but he might play golf.

Ashe was having a good time, too, jet-setting all over the world, dating glamorous women such as Diana Ross and cover girl model Beverly Johnson and, generally speaking, living the good bachelor life. Money was rolling in and he was having a good time, but that's not what Arthur Ashe was all about.[4]

Social Consciousness

Rather, Ashe's new status gave him the opportunity to openly address serious issues he had long wanted to talk about but had not because the time was not right. Finally,

As Ashe became more successful, he enjoyed dating famous women, including Diana Ross (left).

his time had come. His social consciousness was coming to the fore, and his fame, along with his social and political connections, gave him the leverage to move ahead.

One of his first efforts, in collaboration with Donald Dell and Charlie Pasarell in 1968, led to the establishment of the National Junior Tennis League (NJTL), a division of the USTA. A main purpose of the league was to increase the participation of inner-city youths in tennis. Arthur felt that if some of the great black athletes going into basketball, baseball, and football could be diverted into tennis, he might not always be the only black male playing at his level. Today, NJTL has about 200,000 members.[5] This was one of Ashe's earliest ventures into organizations designed to promote the welfare of children. He continued to devote his resources to benefit children throughout his life.

In his tennis life, Ashe traveled to every continent (except Antarctica), either on State Department junkets or on the tournament circuit. He found his trips to Africa especially gratifying, and he was revered in every African country he visited. Stan Smith recalls that at some stops on one trip, Arthur was called the number-one player in the United States. That was a year when Stan Smith was actually number one. Finally, Ashe said jokingly to Smith, "You know, when we do our State Department trip to Alabama, I'll carry your rackets for you." Smith thought that Ashe's government trips were extremely effective diplomacy. "[T]he impact [Arthur had] worldwide on people's impressions of what Americans were like, particularly black Americans . . . that to me was his greatest achievement in life."[6]

Battling Apartheid

There was one country where Ashe could not go, however, and it disturbed him deeply. That was South Africa, where apartheid—total separation of the races—was the official policy of the government. Ashe resolved that he would challenge that policy. This was no longer the laid-back

Arthur Ashe of his carefree college days. Back then, he did not speak up, but now he was sensitized to certain problems of the world, especially those dealing with racial suppression, and he was ready to meet them head-on. In the early 1970s, he switched to an Afro hairstyle, a symbol of black pride and a sign of Ashe's increasing activism in the political and social realm.

Ashe threw down the gauntlet in April 1969 when he was invited to appear before a United Nations committee looking into South Africa's racial segregation policies. He told the committee that he had been denied a visa by that country despite the backing of U.S. Secretary of State William P. Rogers. Ashe called for the banishment of South Africa from the ILTA. Before the year was out, Ashe again applied for a visa, but was again refused although he had been approved to compete by the South African Lawn Tennis Union.[7]

Ashe appealing to the U.N. General Assembly during a hearing about South Africa's apartheid

Ashe was far from being the only force opposing apartheid in sports. In Britain, in particular, there were open anti-apartheid demonstrations during various sporting events, including tennis, rugby, and soccer, protesting participation of South African teams. The Olympic Committee also moved to boycott South Africa, and eventually did so. Pressure by Ashe and others finally caused South Africa to announce a change in the apartheid policy, which would eliminate the color bar in tennis. The move was looked upon with some skepticism from various quarters, and Ashe stated in July 1969 that he would test the policy that year by again applying for a visa so he could take part in the South African Open Championships.[8]

That visa application was also turned down by the South African government, which claimed that Ashe's visit would be political, based on his highly visible stand against apartheid. Ashe retorted that his only purpose was to play in that country's tennis championships, but he knew of course that his presence would be a blow against apartheid. South Africa knew it too, but they were rapidly running out of options. That nation was already in big trouble in international sports, having been barred from the Olympics and a number of other international competitions, including the World Cup. Numerous sports authorities urged the country to admit Ashe, warning that it could face further recriminations.

The pressure brought by Ashe's stand paid further dividends in March 1970, when the South African Davis Cup team was barred from that year's participation. The nation dug itself deeper into its international political hole when it barred Ashe from open participation for a third time in 1971, calling him "persona non grata" (an unacceptable person). However, it did admit two non-white women players—Evonne Goolagong, an Australian Aborigine, and a woman from Japan—because they were higher up on the South African racial scale than African-derived blacks. Ashe issued a statement in response to their latest rebuff, saying he felt "pity" for South Africa.[9]

Finally, in 1972, South Africa eased their restrictions on interracial sports, and they were reinstated in Davis Cup competition. The next year, Ashe got his visa and was registered in the South African Open. The reaction to this was not all good, however. The more militant elements of the U.S. civil rights movement and the South African anti-apartheid movement thought Ashe should refuse to play in South Africa, that he was being used as a token. Ashe was even booed by some disruptive individuals during a speech he gave at Dartmouth University.

Going to South Africa

But Ashe held his ground. After all, the South African government were the ones that backed down. He was getting what he wanted, even to the extent that the stands would be integrated whenever he played. In a press interview he said, "[I]t was one of my conditions that I wouldn't play in front of a segregated audience. So if the audiences are segregated, I won't be walking out there." These were concessions. Ashe steadfastly disagreed with India's Davis Cup team when it refused to play South Africa in the 1974 final, thus letting South Africa become the champion by default. In his confrontation with South Africa, Ashe believed he had turned the situation around. Now, he was using them.[10]

To make his point, he elicited great crowd support from both black and white patrons in winning his first four matches of the tourney, the fourth against native son Cliff Drysdale, who had become Ashe's good friend and who was almost as outspoken against apartheid as Ashe was.

In the final Arthur was matched up against a young upstart who was blazing his way to the top of the tennis hierarchy with great two-handed power strokes. His name was Jimmy Connors. Ashe had played Connors for the first time earlier in the year and greatly respected his game, but not his brash on-court behavior. Despite being heavily favored by the crowd, to the point where it embarrassed Ashe, he lost that day to Connors. It was not the way storybook writers would have ended it, but Ashe was satisfied with his accomplishment in any case. He was the first black male to play center court at the South African Open Championships, and he had made it to the finals. And he won the doubles with Tom Okker, thus becoming the first black male to win a major tennis tournament championship of any kind in South Africa. It was a beginning.[11]

On and off the Court

No doubt Ashe's devotion to causes off the court affected the quality of his game. South Africa was his main focus in the early 1970s, but Ashe wanted to do it all. Stan Smith would say, "He was always concerned about his time and not wasting time. . . . He wasn't the kind to hang around and shoot the breeze."

In 1970, to further his pro tennis career, Ashe, along with Lutz and Pasarell, signed five-year contracts with Lamar Hunt to join his pro tennis league, World Championship Tennis (WCT). In addition to playing tennis, working with corporations, and becoming involved in world politics, Ashe was also becoming deeply embroiled in tennis politics. In 1969, he had helped found the International Tennis Players Association (ITPA) and was its treasurer until that organization was replaced by the Association of Tennis Professionals (ATP) in 1972.

Ashe then served as the first vice president of ATP and later as president. He still felt the sting of discrimination in Richmond that had kept blacks out of the decision-making process, and he was anxious to be a part of the association's administrative machinery. The crisis year for ATP came in 1973 when the association voted to boycott Wimbledon. The move was in support of Nikki Pilic, a Yugoslavian player who was suspended by the ILTF because his national federation claimed he backed out of a commitment to play on their Davis Cup team. The players got a lot of bad press, but with Ashe helping to lead the charge, they held out, and most of the world's top players did not enter Wimbledon that year, including Stan Smith, the defending champ.[12]

Although Ashe's tennis career did not include a lot of major tournament wins in the immediate years after his U.S. Open win, it definitely had its high spots, and he remained continuously in the top rank of players. Most notable perhaps was his victory in the Australian Open Championships in 1970, his second grand slam win. He also stayed on the Davis Cup team, which repeated its 1968 championship in 1969 and 1970. His game may have slipped in 1971, but in 1972 it sharpened again to its best level since 1968. In the 1972 U.S. Open, he again went to the finals, this time to face Ilie Nastase, a Romanian court jokester who was also noted for his nasty temper. Ashe went ahead two sets to one and only had to hold serve to win the fourth set, but the crafty Romanian held on to win that set and the next for the match. Some observers criticized him for letting the match get away, from both himself and the nation. Ashe was disappointed, though as usual his demeanor did not show it. Nastase's on-court clowning may have bothered Ashe, but he made no excuses.[13]

The Connors Rivalry

Ashe had a pretty good year in 1974, but that was the year Connors burned up the circuit, winning the Australian, U.S., and Wimbledon Championships. Through that year, however, a bitter rivalry developed between Ashe and Connors. It was precipitated by a remark Ashe made challenging Connors's patriotism. Connors was young and headstrong, the acknowledged best tennis player in the world, and was very much inclined to go his own way. Ashe wondered why Connors would not join the ATP while benefiting from its activities, and he commented that Connors was "seemingly unpatriotic" because he shunned the Davis Cup team, which had fallen on relatively bad times. Connors was furious about Ashe's view of his patriotism, felt he had been slandered, and initiated a libel suit against the ATP of which Ashe was then president.

The tension between Ashe and Connors provided a most dramatic backdrop for the 1975 All-England tourney.

Connors was again blowing away his competition, but Ashe was coming along too. Some said he was playing the best tennis of his life. Before 1975, he had been dubbed "the world champion runner-up" on the pro circuit. But Ashe changed all that, winning five of seven matches culminating in a Dallas showdown in which he took the WCT crown. His opponent in the finals was nineteen-year-old Bjorn Borg of Sweden, who was already pushing Connors as the next tennis phenom. Ashe won $50,000 plus assorted other items, including the first solid-gold tennis ball, then worth $33,333. His tennis winnings for the year just to that point, were $171,161.[14]

Continuing his streak, Ashe fought his way into the quarterfinals at Wimbledon where he once again met Borg, and with the same result. In the semis he put away Tony Roche, an Australian ace, to set up a final match against the 1974 champ and hottest player in tennis: Jimmy Connors. The feuding between Ashe and Connors gave this match an extra dimension, and the press played it up. To add a little extra twist, Ashe walked out on the court with his Davis Cup jacket on, which was widely interpreted as a dig at Connors for his Davis Cup rebuff.

Ashe had never beaten Connors, but when he walked on the court that day he felt strangely confident. Connors was a huge favorite, but Ashe had prepared for this match as no other. The previous night, he sat down with his friends, including Dennis Ralston, Donald Dell, Marty Riessen, and Charlie Pasarell, and laid out a game plan.

They determined that playing power against power with Connors was insane. Connors was just too strong. It would take finesse to beat him. Ashe later wrote, "Generally . . . I hit the ball *at* him. I didn't want to give him any angles. That's where others have gone wrong. And I wouldn't let Connors hang back. Even on grass he's three times better at the baseline than at net. So I'd dink it straight at him, and force him to come in. Then I'd make him go wide . . . especially on the backhand. . . ."[15]

The strategy worked. He demolished Connors in the

Shaking hands with Jimmy Connors, after Ashe's victory
at Wimbledon

first two sets, 6–1, 6–1. Connors came back to take the third
set, 5–7, but Arthur held to his game plan, winning the
match and Wimbledon, 6–4. The last point came on a smok-
ing serve that Connors returned weakly, allowing Arthur to
slam the winner. His first thought after the win was a sad
one: Dr. Johnson had not lived to see his greatest triumph.
Then Ashe raised a fist toward Donald Dell in the stands, a
sort of victory salute.[16]

At last Ashe could fulfill the dream he had as a
Wimbledon rookie—that he might dance the winner's dance
with the women's champion at the Wimbledon Ball. His
partner at the ball that night was an equally proud Billie

121

Jean King, taking the winner's romp for the sixth time.

At year's end, Arthur Ashe was named the number-one U.S. player and the number-one player in the world. Afterward in an interview with tennis writer Barry Lorge, Arthur said, "I can tell my grandchildren, 'In 1975, I was the best tennis player in the whole world.' "[17] It was not a wish he would fulfill.

Holding the 1975 Wimbledon cup

14

Jeanne and Matters of the Heart

The sporting world buzzed about Ashe's upset win over Connors long after the stadium emptied. *The New Yorker* magazine in its coverage stated that, "Weeks after Wimbledon, tennis buffs were still talking about the match, and it is hard to remember another in the last decade that has been analyzed so carefully, or discussed so frequently over so long a period."[1]

Life on Top

For the moment at least, Ashe was perched on top of the world, the best tennis player in the universe and in a position to do anything he wanted with his life. At this point in time, his "home," or at least the place where he felt most at home was the tennis circuit. He was on the move most of the time and felt quite comfortable in the clubs and hotels where he stayed as well as with the players, who had become a kind of "family." When he wasn't on the circuit, he might be traveling for any of the several corporations with whom he had contractual arrangements. Between these engagements, Ashe usually settled into an apartment he kept in New York City, which he found to be a good base of operations, socially and professionally. His other nesting place was the Doral Country Club in Miami, where he was on staff.[2]

Ashe's cost of living was pretty high at this point. He estimated that it cost him about $25,000 a year to be a touring pro, in addition to his apartment and other expenses. He could afford it, however. His net worth was now estimated at more than $1 million, much of it coming from off-the-court enterprises. Arthur enjoyed the luxuries that money can buy, but he was not extravagant. He liked to feel that he used his money wisely.[3]

Ashe continued to give his time to charities and to support causes he felt strongly about. Shortly after Wimbledon, he and Billie Jean King played a benefit tourney in Washington, D.C., and met President Gerald Ford. Such benefits were now routine, as were the free clinics he gave for inner-city youths. Ashe was also deeply involved in the activities of TransAfrica, an organization designed primarily to fight racism in Africa. After his first trip to South Africa, he decided to set up a foundation to aid promising black South African tennis players. And he helped found an organization called Artists and Athletes Against Apartheid, which he co-chaired with actor/singer Harry Belafonte.[4]

Ashe took care of his mind as well and continued his intellectual pursuits. A favorite writer was Hermann Hesse, whose philosophy, he felt, particularly matched tennis playing because of its emphasis on individualism. He also delved into the works of Robert Ardrey, William Styron, Albert Camus, John Updike, and James Michener. He always hungered for information, sometimes reading two or more newspapers a day and several magazines a week. He even liked to browse through the encyclopedia just for the joy of learning.

Ashe's musical appetite was as varied as it was voracious. On a typical trip, he would take as many as sixty-five musical tapes with him. He might listen to Beethoven and Brahms, or the Beatles and Eric Clapton, or the trumpet playing of Miles Davis and Dizzy Gillespie. And he loved gospel music too. In the visual arts, his particular favorite was Rembrandt. One of Ashe's proudest possessions was a Rembrandt etching entitled *The White Negress*.[5]

A Personal Life

Comfortably well off, sophisticated in the arts, well-traveled with a very bright future, and unmarried, Ashe was the quintessential eligible bachelor. He had dated a number of women but had not come close to marriage after Pat Battles. During the year in which he worked on *Portrait in Motion,* his companion for part of the trip was Kathy Benn, a Jewish-Canadian commercial artist. At the beginning of *Portrait in Motion,* he announces that Kathy Benn, "a beautiful blond," is his girlfriend and that they have grown very close.

They were together for four weeks in Europe, and when she had to return to Toronto, Ashe found the parting difficult. Nevertheless, their relationship was sometimes stormy. After about two years, he suddenly realized the "zing" had gone out of it, and in June 1974, just prior to Wimbledon, he sadly called the relationship off. Watching her leave on the train, he said, was one of the most difficult things he had ever done. That same day he lost in doubles.[6]

Less than two years later, Ashe attended a United Negro College Fund benefit in New York City that turned out to be a most fateful event. A group of photographers were taking Ashe's picture, and one of them happened to catch his eye. She was very attractive, but it was more than that. There had been many attractive women in his life by then. Perhaps it was the simple way she was dressed, just a sweater and jeans, with very light makeup. Or did she remind him of someone? Arthur was intrigued and sought quickly for an opening line: "Photographers are getting cuter these days." It was not a winner.

Fortunately, it did not totally put her off. After the benefit tournament, he had a chance to meet with her again. This time they were able to carry on a conversation, and he was very impressed by her poise and intelligence. The lady that lit Ashe up was twenty-five-year-old Jeanne Moutoussamy.[7]

Ashe was not hasty in his dating. He had been involved in a number of relationships, but he was pretty selective. Billie Jean King would say, "You know he wasn't always out there dating like a crazy man. That's for sure. He was pretty

The engaged couple, Ashe and Jeanne Moutoussamy in 1977

gentle and quiet."[8] But Ashe was on the move constantly so he had to size up situations quickly and act, or the opportunity would be gone. His instincts generally did not betray him. With Jeanne, though, he was smitten instantly. He had always thought he would know when he met the right one, and practically from the first date he knew Jeanne was "it." His schedule, of course, kept him away, but he began calling her virtually every day, no matter where in the world he was. Their relationship took off and never cooled down.

Ashe was thirty-three now and ready. He had told himself that he would not marry until his playing days were over, but such proclamations are subject to revision as circumstances change. When Ashe took Jeanne to meet his father in Gum Springs, the die was cast. She was the first girlfriend he had ever brought to his father's home. Arthur Sr. took one look at Jeanne with her long dark-brown hair, high cheekbones, and light complexion, and told his son that she looked just like his mother. Perhaps Arthur subconsciously caught this resemblance when he first met Jeanne.

Jeanne was from the Moutoussamy family of Chicago. Her father, John, was a noted architect with the firm of Dubin, Dubin and Moutoussamy. Her mother, Elizabeth, was one of eleven children, and she and John had three: John, Claude, and Jeanne. The family roots included East Indian and African-American ancestry. Jeanne was bright and talented—as Arthur found out—and was accepted at Cooper Union in New York City where she earned a B.F.A. in photography. She went on to work in photojournalism, and her photographs appeared in numerous magazines and books, including her own *Daufuskie Island: A Photographic Essay. Viewfinders* is her compilation of the work of black female photographers.[9]

Jeanne and Arthur were alike in many ways. She was strong and independent with an insatiable appetite for learning. Jeanne commented in an interview that "My father will tell you 'Jeanne is going to follow her own mind no matter what anyone says.' " Arthur admired her spirit, and loved her the more for it. In the same interview she was described in these terms: "Everything about her—from her measured, melodic voice to her chiseled, patrician beauty—seems so cool, so unflappable, so serene."[10] Those qualities also might have described Arthur. They were drawn to each other with seemingly inexorable cosmic force, and seven months later, in February 1977, they were married.

Making a Commitment

The wedding was performed by Arthur's friend, the Reverend Andrew Young, a civil rights activist who had been appointed the United Nations ambassador by President Jimmy Carter. Jeanne and Arthur grew together and learned from each other. Arthur often expressed himself in tough, logical terms. He kept his emotions contained. But Jeanne taught Arthur how to express himself emotionally. She also widened Arthur's thinking in areas he had

Arthur and Jeanne were married on February 20, 1977, at the United Nations chapel.

largely ignored. Jeanne was a strong feminist, for instance, and she was not about to put up with any macho nonsense. Arthur required considerable reorientation in that regard. "He was pretty chauvinistic, quite frankly," Billie Jean King would say of the premarital Arthur Ashe. She was referring to his and other American male tennis stars' aversion to practicing with their female counterparts.

The men also kept the women out of their labor movement, and did not garner their support for the Wimbledon boycott. King asked Arthur at one point, "[D]o you want me to get the women organized as well? And he said 'no, we don't need you.' " King could not understand why the men would not want to add women's strength to the movement. She said later,

> That was hard to take. It was very difficult. I was very hurt. It wasn't [just] Arthur. It was . . . everybody [ATP leadership]. You know, no human being likes to be discounted.
>
> What really changed his life, as far as being less chauvinist, was marrying Jeanne, because Jeanne is an unbelievable feminist, and Arthur always told me he would never marry a woman like that. . . . Anyway, I showed up for this women's sports foundation press conference, and who is sitting there but Arthur. And I said, "What are you doing here?" We howled with laughter, and he said, "well it's because of Jeanne," and I said, "Have you been enlightened?" And he replied, "Absolutely . . . I never realized women's sports was getting such a bad deal."[11]

Surgery and a Comeback

Arthur and Jeanne's wedding and reception was a grand affair, but Arthur limped to the altar. Not from fear, but because only a few days before he had surgery on his left heel. The heel had been a problem for him for several years, but it got progressively worse as the calcium deposits grew. Finally he decided on surgery, hoping to extend his playing days. Even during his big Wimbledon win, he had been in pain. The surgery was successful, although he would always feel some discomfort in that heel. Before long he was back on the court, and playing well, if not spectacularly. With Jimmy Connors and Ashe leading the way, the American team had won the World Cup competition in 1976. After his surgery, however, Ashe's world ranking had slipped to 257th. It was a long way back up the ladder, and how high he could climb was anybody's guess.

Come back he did, though, showing his champion's colors. Now he was the grizzled veteran fighting off the fresh, healthy younger players. In 1978, he was again fit enough to play on the Davis Cup, helping the American team regain its championship, the first since 1971. Ashe played a full schedule that year, winning sixty-five of eighty matches, a good average for him. His U.S. ranking went back up to ninth. He trained harder than ever, seeking to extend his glory days as long as possible. In 1979, at thirty-five, Ashe started to show flashes of his old form. No, it wasn't the sheer power game of his youth, and he wasn't as quick on his feet. Now it was more of a head game that included the things he had done to defeat Connors. His tactics carried him into the semifinals at the Australian Open going into 1979, and in January he was entered in the Grand Prix Masters. He battled his way through the quarters and semis and landed in the finals. His opponent was nineteen-year-old John McEnroe, another brash upstart in the Connors's mode.[12]

It was a *High Noon* kind of shootout, youth against age. The run-and-gun warrior was ranked slightly above Ashe in the U.S. standings, but Ashe was the wily old fox. He studied videotapes of McEnroe's previous match and drew up a game plan to befuddle the younger player, who had not to this point won a major singles title. Ashe stood more to the backhand side to receive serve, and he mixed up his game, keeping the favored McEnroe guessing. The crowd was clearly behind Ashe, who surprised them, taking the first set, 7–6. Despite his tender years, McEnroe did not crack, coming back to win the second set, 6–3.

It was all on the line for the third set, and the crowd was now hanging on every stroke. Ashe went ahead, and then he had McEnroe on the ropes, at double match point. He needed to win only one point on his serve to take the championship. One of Ashe's serves went for an ace and would have been the match, but the linesman called it out. McEnroe fought back to break serve and take the game. McEnroe went on to win the match. Ashe may have been defeated, but he had gained great respect from the tennis elite.[13]

An End to Competitive Tennis

Ashe went to the finals in another major tournament, the U.S. Pro Indoor, losing to Jimmy Connors. But it had been a good year so far, and going into the summer, Ashe's U.S. ranking was back up to fifth. Ashe played an Austrian tournament that summer, and after he and Jeanne got back to New York City, he went into a strict training regimen. He also continued to give tennis clinics, including one at the East River Tennis Club on Long Island. At the beginning of August, during one of these clinics, Arthur was taking a break when he suddenly felt a severe and wrenching pain in his chest. He was rushed to the hospital where it was confirmed that he had suffered a heart attack. More than likely he was thinking then of his family history—his mother's death involved heart complications, and his father had survived a couple of heart attacks. Jeanne rushed to the hospital, and while she retained her composure, she must have thought of her own family history of heart problems. Her father had already survived a brush with death, and her brother John was at high risk.

After a thorough analysis of his condition, the doctors confronted Ashe with the news he dreaded to hear. His playing days were over unless he underwent open-heart, bypass surgery. And even then, there was only a slight chance that he would ever return to the professional court. Ashe did not want to undergo surgery. Being the fighter he was, and being otherwise in excellent health, he thought he could beat the disease by other means. So he started taking medication and went on a cholesterol-free diet. He did not smoke, of course, and his physical conditioning was superb. He did well for about two months, but then in Jacksonville, Florida, he started to have heart palpitations. He made the decision then to risk the surgery as a means of prolonging his career.[14]

Arthur Ashe underwent quadruple bypass coronary surgery on December 13, 1979. Just before the surgery, Ashe had announced to the press that he expected to return to tennis, possibly by Easter. Arthur did not return to tennis by April, however. He did not return at all. In March 1980, he and Jeanne had taken a trip to Egypt for business and pleasure. Eager to get back into shape, Ashe decided to go for a run. During the run, he developed chest pains and returned to their hotel. After consulting with a physician friend, Ashe realized that his playing days were over.

The following month, Ashe confirmed publicly that he was retiring from tennis. In his statement he said, "A long time ago in my Sunday school classes I learned that for everything there is a season," and went on to say, "From today on, I will end my nonstop odyssey in search of the perfect serve and retire from competitive tennis." He was thirty-six years old and was without a tennis racket in his hand for the first time since he was six.[15]

A new day was dawning in the life of Arthur Ashe.

15

Retirement Arthur Ashe Style

It was not as though Arthur Ashe did not have enough to do. His off-the-court activities were more than a full-time job for most people. And money was not a problem for the Ashes. He could have cut his commitments in half and still had enough to live comfortably. Jeanne urged him to slow down. She wanted to have more leisure time with him, time to relax and just be together. Jeanne, being a bit of a dynamo herself, enjoyed a lot of activity, but her husband's pace was virtually nonstop. He felt compelled to be busy all the time. His response to breaking away:

> I'm not the vacation type. I don't work a nine-to-five schedule. I put things in my appointment book and organize my days around them. It's my nature to keep busy, but Jeanne thinks I work too much . . . I like to experience as much of life as possible. I've always felt I can sleep and rest when I'm dead; while I'm here, let's get it on and live life to the fullest.[1]

With the Davis Cup Team Again

So Ashe did not rest after retirement. To begin with, his affiliation with tennis was far from over. He couldn't play, but he could coach or manage or be associated with the sport in other ways. Still, he didn't expect that the opportunity would present itself as soon as it did. In fact, in the

Ashe with John McEnroe (right) at a Davis Cup match in 1981

same year Ashe retired, he got word that the president-elect of the USTA, Marvin P. Richmond, wished to see him. In their meeting, Richmond told Ashe that Tony Trabert, current captain of the Davis Cup team, wanted out. He could no longer deal with the tantrums and temperament of the new young breed of players. When Ashe asked who might replace Trabert, Richmond replied, "We want you."

Ashe was overwhelmed. It had always been a matter of great pride for him to play for his country, and captaining the team would be equally as great. Ashe was younger than Trabert, closer in age to the team players, and he felt his "quiet diplomacy" would be effective. Also, Ashe always kept his cool, which was thought to be an ideal quality for the Davis Cup captain, especially with this crew of "hotheads." The U.S. Davis Cup team had won only twice between 1974 and 1980, those two wins coming under Trabert in 1978 (when Ashe played) and in 1979. The next year, the team did not reach the final round. So the squad's fortunes were at rather a low ebb as Ashe took over for the 1981 Cup.

Ashe was determined to field the best Davis Cup team possible during his captaincy. He and Connors had certainly had their differences, but Ashe got him to agree to play. McEnroe was already in the fold. Unlike Connors, the younger McEnroe was committed to Davis Cup play, having been on the team for several years already. Ashe then had managed to put what were possibly the two best tennis players in the world on the Davis Cup. Together with the doubles team of Stan Smith and Bob Lutz, it may have been the most powerful U.S. squad of all time.

To make it all happen, however, Ashe had to deal with their volatile personalities. He proved equal to the task. In that first year, the United States regained the Cup. They won again in 1982 under Ashe, although Connors had left the team. That year, their final tie was against France, led by Yannick Noah, a young French African whom Ashe had seen play on one of his African tours. Impressed with Noah's potential, Ashe helped connect him to the right tennis people, which led eventually to his place on the French team.

Ashe was team captain for five years altogether. Besides his first two championships, his team reached the finals one more time in 1984, but they were stormy years. At one point, when McEnroe lost his temper, even Ashe's patience was broken, and he vowed to forfeit the next match, if Mac's behavior didn't improve. Fortunately, McEnroe reined it in.[2] Ashe did not have stars in his eyes over the new breed of player. He told *World Tennis,* "I don't expect anybody to behave like myself or Bjorn Borg or Chrissie Evert. Those days are gone."[3]

In 1984 Connors returned, but both he and Mac were off their games, and the United States lost in the final to Sweden. The next year without Connors or McEnroe, the team went only to the second round. They might have gone farther, but in that round they faced Germany, which had not been much of a force in tennis. That year, however, the German team boasted the latest tennis *wunderkind,* seven-teen-year-old Boris Becker, who had already won his first Wimbledon. A husky, 6-foot 3-inch (191-cm) gentle giant, he dominated play.[4] Years later, when Becker announced his retirement from major tourneys, a sports columnist gave him the highest acclaim he knew. He said, "No one has given the game the same nobility since Arthur Ashe."[5]

After the 1985 season, Ashe assessed the situation. He had an impressive 13–3 record, but he had not won a championship in his last three tries. The USTA was disappointed, and so was Ashe. Amid reports that he was to be replaced, Ashe resigned his captaincy in October 1985. At the same time, he was offered the position of vice chairman of the Davis Cup committee, which he was happy to accept.

Being Honored

Several months earlier, more honors were given to Arthur Ashe, and yet again they put him in the history books. In July 1985, Ashe became the first African-American male to be inducted into the International Tennis Hall of Fame. Ashe, now forty-two years old, was gratified that he had made it in the first year he became eligible. Looking on proudly were Jeanne, Arthur Sr., and numerous other members of the Ashe and Moutoussamy families.[6] Scarcely a month later, *Tennis* magazine voted him among the top twenty performers of the last two decades, and among the top twenty most influential people in the game. Ashe had been far more than just a player.

The first African-American man inducted into the International
Tennis Hall of Fame, July 1985

Combating More Surgery

Ashe probably could have offered a good excuse for the Davis Cup team's slide in 1983 after two successive championships. Not that he would ever use it as an excuse, but in that year just before he was to go to Wimbledon as an HBO commentator, Ashe's repaired heart again malfunctioned. Before the end of June, Ashe underwent his second open-heart surgery. It was a double bypass this time, but a more difficult surgery because of the scar tissue that had formed after the first operation.

Ashe felt considerably weaker after this encounter, but the doctor said he would regain his strength in a few weeks. On the other hand, if he wanted a quick charge, they could transfuse him with a couple of units of blood. The decision was a no-brainer for Ashe. He wanted to get up and go, so transfusion was the obvious choice. Ashe did feel better right away, but that apparently simple decision added a tragic twist to his life.

Neither retirement nor surgery could slow Ashe down. He had been involved in numerous activities during his Davis Cup captaincy, and his interests continued to expand afterward. He spread himself over several areas, including writing and sports commentary, consulting to various corporations and institutions, teaching, and taking part in various causes about which he felt strongly, such as the anti-apartheid movement, civil rights, education, and others. His role as a TV sports commentator actually went back to the late 1970s when he signed a five-year contract with ABC-TV. One of his first assignments was a documentary that examined the progress of sports integration under apartheid. Later, HBO hired Ashe and Billie Jean King as a team to do commentary on their Wimbledon broadcasts.

Arthur Ashe, the Writer

Ashe was as addicted to writing as he was to tennis. His name was on three books before he retired: *Advantage Ashe*, published in 1967 shortly after he left college, his diary *Portrait in Motion*, published in 1975, and *Getting Started in*

Tennis, in 1979. In 1981, shortly after retirement, *Off the Court,* reflections on his life and career, came out. In addition to book writing, Arthur wrote a bi-weekly feature for the *Washington Post* and did commentary for *The Observer* in London. He was also a consultant for *Tennis* magazine and wrote instructional articles. The articles were later combined and published in book form.

In addition, Ashe also had occasional articles published in *The New York Times.* These were not always about tennis. More often they urged black children to get a good education or promoted higher educational standards for black athletes. He thought blacks should meet the same college standards as whites. He was not in favor of affirmative action and spoke out against it, even though his viewpoint was unpopular with much of the black community.

Corporate Connections

Ashe had long-term associations with numerous corporate clients, and he had maintained his position as the tennis director at the Doral in Miami since 1970. Some of his more enduring corporate work was with Head USA, who named a racket for him, and Le Coq Sportif, whose line of sports clothing he endorsed. There were others too, such as Bristol-Myers, Volvo, and Philip Morris, although Ashe only worked with the non-tobacco products of the latter. Ashe even served for a time as a consultant with the U.S Army to help alleviate a racial crisis among servicemen in Germany.

He said, however, that his most satisfying business association after retirement was with Aetna Life and Casualty Company. Ashe came to know the Aetna executives after they took over sponsorship of the World Cup in 1970. Starting as a consultant in the late 1970s, Ashe worked with the insurance giant on minority recruitment but later went to another level with Aetna. One day in 1982 he got a call for a face-to-face meeting with the company president, and he hadn't a clue as to what it was about. Ashe was afraid that he had committed some enormous blunder. When he strode into the office feeling imperiled, the president looked him in the eye and said, "Arthur, we want you on the board of directors." Taken aback at first, Ashe finally composed himself enough to accept the position. He became the youngest man on the Aetna board, and the only black.[7]

Important Causes

Despite his corporate commitment, Ashe's social consciousness would not let him forget his roots or the causes that needed his strength. Children, youth, and education continued to be a main focus. He had already helped found the NJTL. He followed that in the late 1980s with the Ashe-Bollettieri Cities program (ABC). The program was designed to bring tennis to kids in depressed environments and, in the process, teach them the values and provide them with the training and orientation they would need to move ahead.

They brought in Bob Davis, who now had considerable experience running tennis programs, to manage the organization. He felt it was "the best grass roots program in America. . . . Arthur was a dreamer and he imagined that this tennis program should have a medical component, so we developed the first tennis program we are aware of between a tennis program and a hospital." He went on to say that "academics were a big part of our program; we put many kids through college." Referring to Ashe's appreciation of what he had received through tennis, Davis said, "He was always giving back."[8] Arthur eventually established the Safe Passages Foundation to run ABC and Athletes Career Connection, another program designed to help disadvantaged youth. The latter was, unfortunately, short-lived.

Undaunted and convinced that a growing number of black college athletes needed academic and career guidance, Ashe initiated the African American Athletic Association. Ashe stated that the organization would address "the daunting statistics about increased black involvement in sports and the decline in black academic performance . . ." To run the association, Ashe put together an outstanding board of figures from sports and education, with himself as chair.[9]

Ashe did not just talk and write about the problems of education and blacks. He was always willing to put himself right on the line. Teaching was something he thought he would enjoy doing, but he was never sure of his qualifications, especially in college. He had only a bachelor's degree. He did, however, in the course of time compile a whole armful of doctorate degrees, all honorary. These included honors from Virginia Union University, Trinity College, Bryan College, St. John's University, Princeton University, Dartmouth College, LeMoyne University, Long Island University, and the University of South Carolina.[10] A tempting offer to teach came in 1983 from Yale University, when Arthur was there lecturing on "Collegiate Athletics: A Reappraisal," obviously a favorite subject.

But Ashe turned down the Yale offer, choosing instead to teach a course at Florida Memorial College, a historically black institution. The course he organized and taught was called, "The Black Athlete in Contemporary Society," a subject he felt well qualified to teach. Ashe found out two things very quickly at Florida Memorial: First, these kids, honors students at that, were woefully unprepared for college, especially in terms of writing skills. It reinforced his resolve that black education needs to be stressed more and more. Second, he was astounded at the abysmal lack of resource material available on the subject. By the time he had finished the course, he was determined to fill the void of historic information on black athletes. His course of action thereafter led to his next and most prodigious writing experience: a three-volume collection he called *A Hard Road to Glory: A History of the African-American Athlete.*

So enthused was Ashe in this project that he bypassed seeking a publisher and funded the work himself, including staff salaries, research, and other costs, eventually to the tune of about $300,000. Probably no other book undertaking gave Ashe as much gratification, because it was such a learning experience. His zeal rubbed off on his seven-mem-

141

ber staff, who "combed public and university libraries, personal archives, and the closets, attics and basements of the families of sports legends to gather their material."[11]

Published in 1988, it was an emotional experience for Arthur because, as he said, "[It] dealt so intimately, at almost every stage with both the triumph and tragedy, the elation and suffering of blacks as they met not only the physical challenges of their sport but also the gratuitous challenges of racism."[12]

Ashe's life was rich, rewarding, and extremely full; he had accomplished virtually everything he had set his sights on. Yet, for him and Jeanne there seemed to be something missing, something they had pondered and about which they had to come to a decision: parenthood.

16

❦

Parenthood and a Last Great Match

Having a child is serious step for anyone, but for the Ashes the decision was agonizing. They had to consider the health risks. Billie Jean King commented, "They have heart problems on both sides, and I think doctors basically told them, your chances of having a child with heart problems are very high." There were other considerations too. They were both extremely busy, and a child would require sacrifices from both of them in their careers. Finally, they decided that the experience of parenthood was something they could not pass up in their lives. Considering the health risks to the child, however, they decided against being birth parents.

Life with Camera

In December 1986, the Ashes became the proud adoptive parents of a baby girl. They named her Camera. That was mostly Jeanne's idea, probably because of its relation to photography, but also because she was fond of the male name Cameron. Camera did not have to spend her early childhood in Manhattan, where Arthur had long been a resident. Possibly because they knew Camera was coming, but also because Arthur had tired of the congested uptown Manhattan scene, he and Jeanne had moved to a lovely home in Mount Kisco, a New York City suburb. After the noise and crush of the city, they suddenly had 7 rolling acres (3 hectares) to roam around in and a large house set in the tranquil countryside.

Like most new parents, the Ashes had no idea how much Camera would change their lives. She became the focus of everything they thought and did. Arthur looked forward to fatherhood, but he could not have guessed how wrapped up he would become in his daughter. "She was the jewel of his eye," Stan Smith said. "He may have actually spoiled her a little bit, but you know he wanted to spend all of the time he could with her." Ashe, acknowledging his deep dedication to Camera, wrote, "I had no idea I would love fatherhood as much as I do. I have an acute sense of responsibility for her—to help her, teach, protect her, and (most of all) to love her." Billie Jean King would say, "He loved her, he really loved her. When they

Family life was important to Arthur and Jeanne, so Camera (center) became their main focus.

[later] would come to Wimbledon, he just couldn't wait to hold her hand and take her around."

Billie Jean King also noted other changes in Ashe after Camera entered his life. Referring to his new attitude toward women's rights, she said, "[H]e would come to our women's foundation dinners and, of course, what put him over the edge was . . . when they adopted Camera . . . that put him over. He was totally gone. He was all for girls. . . . You could see that the whole paradigm of his life . . . had been challenged."[1] She also noted another change: "He just flowed with love for her, but what it did was spill over to all of us. Everyone noticed it, how much he changed when Camera came into his life."[2]

Camera, indeed, had added a new dimension to Ashe's life, and he threw himself into his work with renewed energy. He especially became increasingly active in charitable work, estimating in 1988 that he was donating 20 percent of his time to various causes. For instance, he headed up the Black Tennis and Sports Foundation, and for two years he served as National Heart Association program chairman.

He became particularly interested in health-related matters. His own health now became an even greater concern to him. He wanted to see Camera grow up, and he knew his heart condition put him at high risk. He cut all high-fat foods out his diet, and he reduced his cholesterol level to a relatively safe 140. He also adhered to an exercise routine, including walking and bike riding.[3] In terms of how a heart patient should conduct himself, Ashe followed an almost model life. And with Camera now part of the picture, his spirits ran high and he was about as happy as he had ever been.

A New Challenge

In the late summer of 1988, the Ashe family decided to have a quick weekend respite before the whirlwind activities of the U.S. Open began. They chose a gorgeous resort on Lake George where Ashe had attended a meeting with the Aetna board, a truly inspiring spot. Returning from breakfast one morning, Ashe attempted to make a phone call but found that he couldn't. He could not move the fingers of his right hand. It was a frightening experience, and Ashe did not know what to make of it. Had his hand somehow fallen asleep? Had he bumped it? Or was this a mini-stroke? But he felt fine otherwise. He and Jeanne decided to wait it out a day and see how his hand responded after they returned home from the resort.

When next day brought no improvement, they knew that Ashe needed to see a doctor immediately. They first sought out a physician they knew at the local Mount Kisco medical center. Ashe walked in with his hand hanging limp from his arm. The doctor took one look, asked a few questions, and then ordered an immediate CAT scan of the brain, the likely source of Ashe's problem. The scan showed that something was affecting the left side of the brain (which controls the right side of the body). The doctor could not make an immediate diagnosis and recommended that Arthur see a specialist, a neurologist.

Following through, Ashe, now shaken with anxiety, sought out a neurologist at New York Hospital. That physician could not make an immediate diagnosis either but said that it was probably some kind of infection. He recommended a biopsy—surgically going into the brain, removing the infected tissue, and analyzing it. He did not think they needed to act immediately, but Ashe, typically, went for quick action. "Let's go in," he said. Preparations were made then for the surgery, including a spinal tap and blood test. Ashe heard the results of the tests from his two close physician friends, Eddie Mandeville and Doug Stein, and with Jeanne in the room. It was a surprise and a shocker that would once again entirely change the course of his life.

Arthur Ashe was HIV-positive.

Still reeling from that drastic news, Ashe had the brain surgery and, after lab analysis of the tissue, received yet another medical bombshell. The infection in his brain was something called toxoplasmosis, not always a serious disease in itself, but in the presence of the HIV virus it was a strong indicator of the condition that directly results from HIV. That condition is called Acquired Immune Deficiency Syndrome, more popularly known as AIDS. Ashe was not only HIV-positive, he had full-blown AIDS.

How did Arthur Ashe, living an exemplary, healthy lifestyle, contract AIDS? Most AIDS victims contract the disease one of two ways: through the exchange of bodily fluids either from an infected partner during sexual intercourse or by sharing needles with an infected intravenous drug user. However, there is another way to contract the HIV virus. Some people are accidentally transfused with contaminated blood received after surgery or because they are hemophiliacs. That was the case for Arthur Ashe. When he approved a transfusion to get moving faster after his 1983 surgery, he had received contaminated blood. If the operation had taken place two years later, it is unlikely that he would have contracted the virus because screening for HIV began in 1985. It was the second bad health card Ashe had been dealt: a bad heart and now AIDS.

But what about Jeanne? And Camera? It was one thing for this lethal infection to strike Arthur, but what about his wife and child? Jeanne had been exposed since 1983, five years of contact. Camera had been exposed for more than two years, although the threat to her was minimal because Arthur was not her biological father. The two were quickly tested and, to everyone's great relief, both were HIV-negative. The worst had not happened. Arthur could handle his own condition, but how could he have dealt with either of the two people he loved most in the world having this dreaded disease, knowing he had passed it on? At least he didn't have to think about that.[4]

Getting on with Life

For the time being, outwardly nothing changed for the Ashes. A few of their closest friends knew of Arthur's condition, but that was it. Their lives would go on as normally as possible for now. But on a personal basis, Ashe, reflecting an undaunted spirit, would attack his problem in every way he knew how. Learning about the disease, its history, and the available therapies was part of the strategy. Cooperating with a team of doctors was another part. He began a regimen of medication and therapies and followed it scrupulously. He took up to thirty pills per day. Stan Smith saw an irony in this. When he and Ashe played together, Stan occasionally took a salt pill or possibly an aspirin, while Ashe was proud that he never took a pill for any reason. Now Ashe, quite literally, lived on pills.[5]

Ashe carried on with his various projects, still keeping many balls in the air at once. He just considered AIDS one more ball he had to juggle. He kept his commitments to his corporate associates, continued his sportscasting for HBO and ABC, and carried on with his writing for the *Washington Post* and other journals. Yet another writing challenge came his way when HBO decided to present a docudrama version of the Ashe's *Hard Road to Glory*. The producers asked Ashe to write the television version. The project delivered another honor to Ashe: an Emmy Award for writing. In 1989, he became part of a combine that purchased the Denver Nuggets basketball franchise, the first all-black ownership of a major sports franchise.[6]

But tragedy was not yet through with Ashe. In March 1989, he received a fateful phone call from his stepsister. She announced what Arthur had long dreaded to hear: his father had died of heart complications. Besides his immediate family, no one meant as much to Arthur than Arthur Ashe, Sr., and he loved him dearly. "My heart withstood the shock," he said in *Days of Grace*, "but I cried and cried when I heard the news. Dominating, stern, protective, my father had loved me and taken care of me when I needed him most."

Ashe persevered in his efforts to help black youth to succeed. It was in 1990 that he launched the Safe Passage Foundation and in 1991 that the African American Athletic Association had its kickoff. And Ashe also kept going in his struggle against the tyranny of apartheid. In 1989, he pleaded with the ATP not to hold tournaments in South Africa as they were planning to do. Nelson Mandela, he said, wanted the boycott upheld. The ATP complied.

Ashe did not know how much time he had left, but he wanted to go back to South Africa at least once more. In 1991, he got his wish. He was invited to join a delegation of African-Americans who had been invited there by Mandela. The African leader was released from jail after twenty-seven years, and there had been a partial dismantling of apartheid. Ashe thanked God he was able to witness it personally. He felt gratified that his efforts on behalf of the oppressed South African blacks had counted for something—even though there was still a way to go.

In 1992, some three and a half years after the diagnosis, the outside world was still not aware that Ashe had AIDS. This was a quite amazing feat, considering that many of his personal friends knew, that the information had spread to some degree in the tennis world and of course within the immediate medical community. Even some people in the media knew or had heard the rumors. Billie Jean King commented that "We at HBO knew for four years that he had AIDS. He didn't realize we all knew. In fact, we were able to keep it quiet for four years. We never told anybody."[7] One thing Ashe's humanity and character had bought over the years was respect, and it won him several years of privacy. Sooner or later, of course, this was bound to end.

Telling the News

One day in April 1992, a reporter from *USA Today* came to visit Ashe. He was Doug Smith, a black boyhood friend. Ashe looked forward to a nice chat with his old buddy, kicking around stories of their youthful days. It sort of started out that way, but Smith rather abruptly changed the subject and stepped into his reporter's role. Smith hit Ashe with the question that he feared someday would come. Smith's editors had heard the rumors and now wanted Ashe to confirm or deny: Did he have AIDS? Ashe could have denied it but he didn't want to lie. He knew his cover had been blown. Life for him and his family would now change immeasurably.

Ashe was only evasive at first, bargaining for time. Because he had not confirmed the story, *USA Today* could not go to press with it immediately without further checking. Ashe first wanted to tell all of his close friends and relatives what was going on, and then he wanted to release the news to the media on his own terms. He wanted time to prepare a statement that would tell the story thoroughly and accurately so there would be no speculation. The best solution, he and Jeanne thought, was to hold a press conference. Ashe appealed to the people at HBO, with whom he was on familiar terms, to set up the conference in their midtown Manhattan offices. They agreed and made the arrangements.[8] On April 8, 1992, Arthur Ashe met the press.

With television cameras rolling and media cameras flashing, Ashe read his statement to the press. It recounted how he had contracted AIDS and why he had kept it a private matter. He thanked those who knew for not spreading the word. Even he seemed somewhat baffled that it had not come out earlier. He said, "What I came to feel about a year ago was that there was a silent and generous conspiracy to assist me in maintaining my privacy. This has meant a great deal to me and Jeanne and Camera."

The name Camera barely got out. His voice cracked at the mention of her name as he was overcome with emotion. Tears streamed from his eyes. Jeanne came to his side and finished reading the reference to Camera—how the revelation of her father's illness would affect her and how they would deal with it to protect her. Ashe then came back to the podium and spoke briefly about how he resented having been pressured by *USA Today* to make public a matter that he felt should have remained entirely private. Many in the media, it turned out subsequently, agreed with him. He then took a battery of reporters' questions.

The news had leaked well before the press conference. That morning Ashe had received well-wishing calls from President George Bush and from Virginia Governor L. Douglas Wilder. Letters also came from former Presidents Richard Nixon and Gerald Ford. Many, many more calls and letters would come later that day and in the weeks and months to come.

Fighting AIDS

What of course happened immediately was that Ashe was thrust into the forefront of the battle against AIDS. He was not the first sports celebrity to find himself in this position. Only a few months earlier, the great Los Angeles Lakers basketball player Earvin "Magic" Johnson had announced he was HIV-positive, and promptly joined the crusade against AIDS. At the press conference, Ashe implied that he might work with Magic and would join the President's Commission on AIDS.

Almost anybody who knew Ashe could have guessed that once he took up the sword against AIDS, he would throw himself into the fray with a vengeance. Not willing to just give lectures and write articles, for which he was now in great demand, he began at once to organize his own association for launching an offensive against the disease. It was to be called the Arthur Ashe Foundation for the Defeat of AIDS.

Fund-raising for the foundation began with a tennis gala the day before the 1992 U.S. Open was to begin at Flushing Meadow, where the event had moved from Forest Hills. Arthur was concerned that his event might be lost against the limelight of the Open, that people might not show up or the tennis stars would back out. His fears were unwarranted. A huge crowd showed up to see the brightest stars of tennis play exhibitions. The inaugural event brought $114,000 to the foundation.

The Haitian Cause

Only a few days after the Open, Ashe again engaged himself in international politics. There was to be a demonstration at the White House to protest administration policy to reject Haitian refugees fleeing their country. Officials said that the Haitians were rejected because they were fleeing economic conditions rather than political persecution. Ashe

Ashe was never afraid to take a stand for the right cause, even if it meant being arrested, as he was during a demonstration for Haitian refugees in 1992.

strongly opposed the policy, which he felt was racist, and joined the demonstration. In the process he was arrested. A news photo showed Arthur being led away in handcuffs. He appeared thinner and somewhat frailer than usual but in high spirits. It was not his first arrest. He had been taken into custody once before in 1985, protesting apartheid at the South African Embassy. Both arrests were of a few hours' duration.[9]

The Haitian experience apparently took its toll on Ashe, because the next day he had another heart attack. Rushed to the hospital, he was quickly treated, and tests were administered. The tests showed no new damage, and Arthur returned home after about a week. He resolved he would not curtail his activities, unless he was physically incapable of carrying on.

Working with Children

Ashe continued his lecturing, his talks now relating mostly to AIDS, and he helped initiate another project in December 1992, the Arthur Ashe Institute for Urban Health in association with a Brooklyn hospital. While at the facility, he visited the children's ward and was deeply touched that the children, also suffering from AIDS, had made a banner welcoming him. He told them that he knew what they were going through because he too had AIDS. A few days earlier, on December 1, 1992, Ashe had addressed the United Nations in a plea for better understanding of AIDS and a greater effort on the part of all nations to eradicate the disease. He called the address "the most significant of my life."[10]

More Projects

Ashe was also working furiously on another long-range writing project. This would be his memoir, *Days of Grace*, which he was writing in collaboration with Arnold Rampersad, Woodrow Wilson Professor of Literature at Princeton University. It would present his thoughts and ideas on a whole range of subjects, including racism, children, education, his experiences with heart disease and AIDS, family, religion, and more.

In 1992, a whole bounty of awards and honors were presented to Ashe, mainly for his humanitarian work. They included the Helen Hayes Award, the first annual AIDS Leadership Award of the Harvard AIDS Institute, the American Sportscasters Sports Legend Award, and, perhaps most notably, he was named Sportsman of the Year by *Sports Illustrated*.

Final Moments

Around Christmas of that year, Ashe was not feeling so well. Still, he enjoyed the holiday with Camera and Jeanne, and then the family packed up and headed for the Florida sun. Arthur felt well enough to get in a few rounds of golf, but by the start of 1993 he had developed a high fever, chills, and shortness of breath. Fearing a serious complication, they quickly packed up and returned to New York. Ashe went directly to the hospital, where he underwent a battery of tests and examinations. Finally the diagnosis came, and it was what Ashe feared. He had developed a form of pneumonia to which AIDS patients are particularly vulnerable, and which can have dire consequences.

Although the doctor said that this bout of pneumonia was not particularly serious, Ashe never really recovered from it. Only a few weeks later, on February 6, 1993, Arthur Ashe, Jr., tennis champion and humanitarian, was dead.

The world mourned.

Eulogies overflowed in the media over the next several days. On February 10, Ashe's body was laid to rest in his hometown of Richmond, Virginia. Some 6,500 people attended the funeral service. Two days later, there was a memorial service in New York City at the Cathedral of St. John the Divine. The mourners included the best-known people of the tennis world, as well as many African-Americans and others whose lives Ashe had touched in one way or another. The eulogies were eloquent and rich with memories of him. They included reflections by New York

Jeanne Moutoussamy-Ashe with Reverend Jesse Jackson, pausing before her husband's casket at his funeral in Richmond, Virginia, February 10, 1993

City Mayor David Dinkins, Billie Jean King, Charles Pasarell, Stan Smith, U.S. Senator Bill Bradley, and Donald Dell.

Perhaps no one captured the spirit of Arthur Ashe better than his dear friend Charlie Pasarell:

> *No man has ever loved a family more than Arthur loved his family. No man has ever loved his friends more than Arthur loved his friends. And yes, it can be said that no man loved all humankind more than Arthur did. That gift of love is Arthur's great virtue. So on this day, I simply want to say to my great friend, I love you, Arthur.*[11]

In 1996, a statue of Arthur Ashe was unveiled on Monument Avenue in Richmond, Virginia—an avenue that had been reserved for the statues of Civil War confederate generals. It may be the final victory of his life that in the city that would not let him play with whites, Arthur Ashe would bring integration to these icons of the Confederacy.

Controversy had raged over both the form and placement of the statue. Art critics argued over the aesthetics of the piece, such as the positioning of the outstretched arms and the way the books and tennis racket were being held. Both black and white factions argued over the placement of the statue on Monument Avenue—blacks claiming that he was above the company of racist Confederate leaders, and whites protesting the integration of the avenue. Eventually, the sculptor, Paul DiPasquale, made changes to satisfy the artistic concerns. But the City Council held firm on the placement of the statue, which, after some internal disputes, received the blessing of closer members of Ashe's family.

Jeanne Moutoussamy-Ashe, however, did not agree to

the location and did not attend the unveiling ceremony in July 1996. She believed that her husband would have wished the statue to be placed in front of an African-American Sports Hall of Fame, which was not yet constructed.[12] The city did agree to move the statue to that location upon completion of the hall. Referring to the statue's present site, former Governor L. Douglas Wilder, Virginia's first black governor since Reconstruction, stated that Monument Avenue "is now an avenue for all people."[13]

Arthur Ashe has received many awards posthumously. Among them, the Olympic Order (the first awarded to a non-Olympian) and the Medal of Freedom, the highest U.S. civilian honor, presented by President Bill Clinton.

The world will not soon forget this exemplary representative of the human spirit.

Source Notes

——— ∿ ———

Preface

1. Arthur Ashe and Arnold Rampersad, *Days of Grace* (New York: Ballantine Books, 1993), pp. 213–216.
2. Virginia Glass, interview with the author, September 3, 1997.
3. Arthur Ashe Kids' Day, narration, August 23, 1997.

Introduction

1. *Inside Tennis* (March 1993), p. 13.
2. *Chicago Tribune* (August 30, 1997), section 3, p. 1.
3. *The New York Times* (February 8, 1993), p. C4.

Chapter 1

1. Arthur Ashe, *Advantage Ashe* (New York: Coward-McCann, 1967), p. 19.
2. Greater Richmond Chamber of Commerce, "Richmond," *The Metropolitan Richmond Visitor's Guide*.
3. *Days of Grace*, p. 139; *Newsweek* (22 February 1993), p. 61.
4. Arthur Ashe with Neil Amdur, *Off the Court* (New York: The New American Library, 1981), p. 19.
5. Ibid., pp. 15–19.
6. Ibid., p. 18.
7. *Advantage Ashe*, p. 13.
8. Arthur Ashe with Frank Deford, *Arthur Ashe: Portrait in Motion*, revised edition (New York: Carroll Graf Publishers/Richard Gallen, 1993), pp. 207, 208.

9. Ibid., p. 160.
10. *Advantage Ashe,* p. 18.
11. *Portrait in Motion,* p. 159.
12. John McPhee, "Levels of the Game," *The New Yorker* (June 7, 1969), pp. 91, 92.

Chapter 2

1. *Portrait in Motion,* p. 224.
2. John McPhee, p. 68.
3. *Off the Court,* p. 36.
4. *Advantage Ashe,* p. 14.
5. Bob Davis, interview with the author, July 1997.
6. Tennis USTA (July 1991), pp. 11, 12.
7. *Advantage Ashe,* p. 20.

Chapter 3

1. *Off the Court,* pp. 25, 26.
2. John McPhee, part 1, p. 97.
3. *Advantage Ashe,* p. 44.
4. John McPhee, part 1, p. 91.
5. *Off the Court,* p. 28.
6. *Richmond Times-Dispatch* (February 11, 1993), p. A11.
7. *Off the Court,* pp. 47, 48.
8. *Portrait in Motion,* p. 148.
9. Ibid., pp. 3, 4
10. *Days of Grace,* pp. 318–320.
11. *Off the Court,* pp. 36–38.
12. John McPhee, part 1, p. 99.
13. Ibid.
14. *Portrait in Motion,* pp. 56–57.

Chapter 4

1. *Advantage Ashe,* pp. 23, 24.
2. *Off the Court,* p. 40.

3. *Advantage Ashe,* pp. 30, 31.
4. John McPhee, part 1, p. 76.
5. Bob Davis, interview with the author.
6. *Advantage Ashe,* p. 26.
7. John McPhee, part 1, p. 59.
8. Ibid., pp. 60–61.
9. Bob Davis, interview with the author.
10. *Portrait in Motion,* p. 225.

Chapter 5

1. Bob Davis, interview with the author.
2. *Advantage Ashe,* p. 25.
3. John McPhee, part 2, p. 76.
4. *Off the Court,* pp. 41, 42.
5. Ibid., p.46.
6. *Advantage Ashe,* pp. 30–37.
7. John McPhee, part 1, p. 98.
8. *Off the Court,* p. 81.
9. *Advantage Ashe,* pp. 37–42.

Chapter 6

1. *Advantage Ashe,* pp. 44–45.
2. Ibid.
3. *Arthur Ashe: Citizen of the World,* Home Box Office, 1994.
4. Virginia Glass, interview with the author.
5. *Arthur Ashe: Citizen of the World.*
6. Ibid.
7. *Off the Court,* p. 47.
8. *Advantage Ashe,* p. 46.
9. *Portrait in Motion,* p. 94.
10. *Advantage Ashe,* p. 47.
11. *Off the Court,* p. 50.
12. *Portrait in Motion,* p. 94.
13. *World Tennis* (June 1978), p. 73.
14. *Advantage Ashe,* p. 51.

Chapter 7

1. *Off the Court*, p. 67.
2. John McPhee, part 1, p. 79.
3. *Off the Court*, p. 54.
4. *World Tennis* (August 1961), p. 70.
5. *Arthur Ashe: Citizen of the World*.
6. *Off the Court*, p. 60.
7. Ibid., p. 55.
8. *Days of Grace*, p. 46
9. *Advantage Ashe*, p. 55.
10. Ibid., p. 56.
11. *Off the Court*, p. 82.
12. *Advantage Ashe*, p. 70.
13. *World Tennis* (October 1962), p. 34.

Chapter 8

1. *Off the Court*, p. 91.
2. *World Tennis* (July 1963), p. 48.
3. *Advantage Ashe*, p. 116.
4. *Off the Court*, p. 70.
5. Ibid., p. 72.
6. *Advantage Ashe*, pp. 118, 119.
7. *World Tennis* (August 1963), pp. 30, 33, 47.
8. *Advantage Ashe*, p. 120.
9. Ibid., p. 168.
10. *Days of Grace*, p. 66.
11. *Advantage Ashe*, p. 68.
12. *World Tennis* (November 1963), p. 71.

Chapter 9

1. *World Tennis*, January 1964, p. 25.
2. *Off the Court*, pp. 89–90.
3. *World Tennis* (May 1964), p. 23, 83, 84, 85.
4. Ibid. (August 1964), pp. 17, 79, 80.
5. *Advantage Ashe*, pp. 64, 65, 124–128.

Chapter 10

1. *Advantage Ashe*, pp. 131–133.
2. Ibid., p. 133
3. *World Tennis* (September 1963), p. 46.
4. *The New York Times Magazine* (January 2, 1966), p. 21.
5. *Advantage Ashe*, p. 134.
6. *Off the Court*, p. 94.
7. *World Tennis* (December 1995), pp. 15–17.

Chapter 11

1. *Advantage Ashe*, pp. 9, 11.
2. Ibid., pp. 11, 13.
3. *The New York Times* (March 19, 1966), p. 14; *Off the Court*, p. 81.
4. Alan Trengrove, *The Story of the Davis Cup* (London: Stanley Paul, 1985), pp. 226, 228, 229, 454–455.
5. *Off the Court*, p. 98.
6. *USTA Tennis Yearbook*, pp. 403, 462.
7. *The New York Times* (March 31, 1968), p. V1; (April 23, 1968), p. 52.

Chapter 12

1. *Off the Court*, p. 102.
2. *The New York Times* (August 25, 1968), pp. 1, 78; (November 19, 1968), p. 19.
3. Alan Trengrove, p. 234.
4. *The New York Times* (August 26, 1968), p. 51.
5. Ibid. (August 29, 1968), p. 2.
6. *World Tennis* (November 1968), pp. 19–31.
7. *The New York Times* (September 10, 1968), pp. 1, 51
8. *Off the Court*, pp. 108–114.
9. *The New York Times* (September 10, 1968), p. 1.
10. *Ebony* (November 1968), p. 65.
11. *Off the Court*, p. 115.
12. Ibid., pp. 116–123.

Chapter 13

1. *Ebony* (November 1968), p. 68.
2. *Days of Grace*, p. 201.
3. *Off the Court*, pp. 130, 131.
4. Ibid., pp. 86, 87.
5. Donald Dell, *Arthur Ashe: A Spirit Larger than a Stadium*, Web Site: Athlete Network.
6. Stan Smith, interview with the author.
7. *The New York Times* (April 16, 1969), p. 7.
8. Ibid. (July 29, 1969), p. 31; (July 30, 1969), p. 32.
9. Ibid. (January 29, 1970), p. 1; (March 24, 1970), p. 1; (February 25, 1971), p. 51.
10. *Days of Grace*, pp. 114, 117, 118.
11. *Portrait in Motion*, pp. 133–138.
12. *Off the Court*, pp. 138–139.
13. *The New Yorker* (October 7, 1972), pp. 133–134.
14. *The New York Times* (May 12, 1975), p. 33; Tennis (August 1975), p. 51.
15. *Portrait in Motion*, p. 275.
16. *Off the Court*, p. 175.
17. *Tennis* (April 1993), p. 113.

Chapter 14

1. *The New Yorker* (October 13, 1975), p. 120.
2. Ibid., p. 128.
3. *Ebony* (November 1975), pp. 146, 148.
4. *Days of Grace*, pp. 121, 122.
5. Ibid., pp. 39, 314.
6. *Portrait in Motion*, pp. 2, 3, 76, 77, 223, 226, 254.
7. *Off the Court*, pp. 181, 182.
8. Billie Jean King, interview with the author, July 9, 1997.
9. *Black Women in America: An Historical Encyclopedia* (Bloomington: Indiana University Press, 1994), volume II, pp. 824–825.
10. *Ebony* (October 1993), pp. 28, 34.
11. Billie Jean King, interview with the author, July 9, 1997.

12. *World Tennis* (April 1979), pp. 44, 45.
13. *The New York Times* (January 15, 1979), p. C6.
14. *Off the Court,* pp. 2, 8–12, 200–203.
15. *The New York Times* (April 17, 1980), section II, p. 20.

Chapter 15

1. *Off the Court,* p. 3.
2. *Days of Grace,* pp. 67, 68, 69, 86–88.
3. *World Tennis* (February 1984), p. 73.
4. *Days of Grace,* pp. 108, 109.
5. *Chicago Tribune,* Sports (July 1997), p. 1.
6. *Jet* (August 12, 1985), p. 56.
7. *Days of Grace,* pp. 205–208.
8. Bob Davis, interview with the author, July 1997.
9. *Days of Grace,* p. 286.
10. UCLA Athletics, Media Relations.
11. *Ebony* (February 1989), p. 30.
12. *Days of Grace,* p. 194.

Chapter 16

1. Interviews with the author.
2. *Arthur Ashe: Citizen of the World.*
3. *Tennis* (September 1988), pp. 53, 54.
4. *Days of Grace,* pp. 218–227.
5. Stan Smith, interview with the author.
6. *Black Enterprise* (April 1993), p. 16.
7. Billie Jean King, interview with the author.
8. *Days of Grace,* pp. 6–17.
9. *The New York Times* (September 5, 1992), p. 20; (October 25, 1992), p.4.
10. *Days of Grace,* p. 301.
11. *Arthur Ashe: Citizen of the World.*
12. *The New York Times* (January 4, 1996), p. A14.
13. *Jet* (July 29, 1996), pp. 46–48.

For Further Information

———— ↶ ————

Books

Ashe, Arthur. *Arthur Ashe's Tennis Clinic.* Norwalk, CT: Golf Digest/Tennis, 1981.

Ashe, Arthur. *A Hard Road to Glory: The History of the African-American Athlete,* 3 volumes. New York: Warner Books, 1988.

Ashe, Arthur, with Neil Amdur. *Off the Court.* New York: New American Library, 1981.

Ashe, Arthur, with Frank Deford. *Portrait in Motion.* New York: Carroll & Graf Publishers/Richard Gallen, 1993.

Ashe, Arthur, Jr., as told to Clifford George Gewecke, Jr. *Advantage Ashe.* New York: Coward-McCann, 1967.

Ashe, Arthur, with Alexander McNab. *Arthur Ashe on Tennis.* New York: Alfred A. Knopf, 1995.

Ashe, Arthur, and Arnold Rampersad. *Days of Grace.* New York: Ballantine Books, 1993.

Ashe, Arthur, with Louie Robinson. *Getting Started in Tennis.* New York: Atheneum/SMI, 1979.

Collins, Bud. *My Life with the Pros.* New York: Dutton, 1989.

Collins, Bud, and Zander Hollander, editors. *Bud Collins' Modern Encyclopedia of Tennis.* New York: Doubleday, 1980.

McPhee, John. *Levels of the Game.* New York: Farrar, Straus & Giroux, 1969.

Moutoussamy-Ashe, Jeanne. *Daddy and Me.* New York: Alfred A. Knopf, 1993.

Quackenbush, Robert. *Arthur Ashe and His Match with History.* New York: Simon and Schuster, 1994.

Robinson, Louie, Jr. *Arthur Ashe: Tennis Champion.* New York: Doubleday, 1967.

Trengrove, Alan. *The Story of the Davis Cup.* London: Stanley Paul, 1985.

Weissberg, Ted. *Arthur Ashe: Tennis Great.* New York: Chelsea House, 1991.

Wright, David K. *Arthur Ashe: Breaking the Color Barrier in Tennis.* Springfield, NJ: Enslow Publishers, 1996.

USTA Tennis Yearbook. Lynn, MA: H.O. Zimman, Inc., Annual Editions.

Videotapes

Arthur Ashe: Citizen of the World, Home Box Office, 1994.
A Hard Road to Glory, Home Box Office, 1988.

Organizations and Publications

American Tennis Association
8100 Cleary Boulevard., Suite 1007
Plantation, FL 33324
Albert Tucker, executive director

Inside Tennis magazine
3561 Lakeshore Avenue
Oakland, CA 94610

International Tennis Hall of Fame
Newport Casino
194 Bellevue Avenue
Newport, RI 02840

Tennis magazine
5220 Park Avenue
Trumbull, CT 06611

United States Tennis Association
70 West Red Oak Lane
White Plains, NY 10604-3602

Internet Sites

Black History/Virginia Profiles: Arthur Ashe
http://www.gatewayva.com/pages/bhistory/1997/ashe.htm
Provides biographical information and commentary on Ashe's life. Also features a timeline and photographs.

CNN/SI—Arthur Ashe
http://cnnsi.com/tennis/features/1997/arthurashe/
profile.html
Provides a profile from Sports Illustrated's *fortieth anniversary issue. Also features a photo gallery, a biography, a look at the Arthur Ashe Stadium, and other* Sports Illustrated *articles about Ashe.*

Life Heroes Hall of Fame: Arthur Ashe
http://pathfinder.com/Life/heroes/newsletters/nlashe.htm
Sponsored by Life *magazine, this site offers a profile of Arthur Ashe. Provides links to other heroes, as well as other Ashe sites.*

World Sports Humanitarian Hall of Fame: Arthur Ashe
http://netnow.micron.net/%7hallfame/ashe.htm
Includes a profile of Arthur Ashe, along with a list of his career highlights.

Acknowledgments

———— ℘ ————

The life of Arthur Ashe was at once a fascinating and difficult subject to deal with because of the complexity of the
man. He lived a life of multiple dimensions, which twisted
and turned and split off in many directions. Whether or not
this work captures the true spirit of Arthur Ashe will be for
the reader to decide. The extent of its success, however, is
directly related to several factors and the cooperation of
many people who graciously contributed to the project.

First and foremost, there was Arthur Ashe himself,
who wrote extensively, covering all the facets of his own
life and expressing his feelings on a whole range of subjects relating to tennis and other topics important to him.
Those of us who have seen fit to explore this man's life will
be forever thankful that he wrote about himself so thoroughly and honestly.

The view from within is a treasure, but we also have to
see how others viewed him and measure the effect he had
on those who knew him. I extend special thanks to Ashe's
associates who granted interviews: Stan Smith, former
number-one player and the current touring pro at the Sea
Pines resort in Hilton Head, South Carolina; Billie Jean
King, also a former number-one player, who knew Ashe
during his playing days and as a commentator for HBO
and is currently the director of World Team Tennis; Bob
Davis, one of Ashe's fellow players at Dr. Johnson's camp,
later a business associate, and now president and CEO of
Black Dynamics, Inc.; and Virginia Glass, whose two sons
were at Dr. Johnson's camp with Ashe, and who housed
Ashe during his early tournaments at Forest Hills, New

York, served as president of the American Tennis Association (ATA), and now is also involved in the United States Tennis Association (USTA).

I received vital assistance from other sources as well: Christine Meyers, formerly of USTA Southwest; Page Crossland, USTA communications director; Merry Kelly, *Tennis USTA* editor; Mark Young, public relations for the International Hall of Fame; Albert Tucker, ATA executive director; Nadia Gutowski, public relations, and Janet Schwarz, reference librarian, Virginia Historical Society; and the staff of UCLA media relations.

My thanks to Lawrence Bowman at the Scottsdale (Arizona) Public Library for his research help; to the Chicago Public Library for their extensive newspaper and publication files; and to the DePaul University library for its vintage collection of *World Tennis* magazines. Relevant source material was provided by Jonathan Rosenthal at the Museum of Television and Radio in New York City and Bruce Dumont, director of the Museum of Broadcast Communications, Chicago.

A special thanks to Bob Coscarelli, Jamie Howard, and Charlton Burch for their technical assistance in a pinch, as well as to Jessica Martin and the PGI Scottsdale office for allowing me some working space at a crucial time.

Finally, I should mention the superb transcribing work of Jaime Cole and Debbie Taylor, whose efforts eased the task before me.

MARVIN MARTIN
MAY 1998

Index

———— ♊ ————

173

175

About the Author

Marvin Martin was born in South Bend, Indiana, but has spent most of his life in Chicago. He served as a sergeant in the U.S. Army and earned a B.A. in English at Roosevelt University before starting his career as a copywriter. Martin then went on to work in editorial positions for World Book Encyclopedia and Encyclopaedia Britannica. Now retired, he writes for a number of publications including the *Chicago Tribune*. He is a board member of the Rochelle Lee Fund, a nonprofit educational institution. His first book, *The Beatles: Music Was Never the Same*, was published by Franklin Watts in 1996.